Delaware

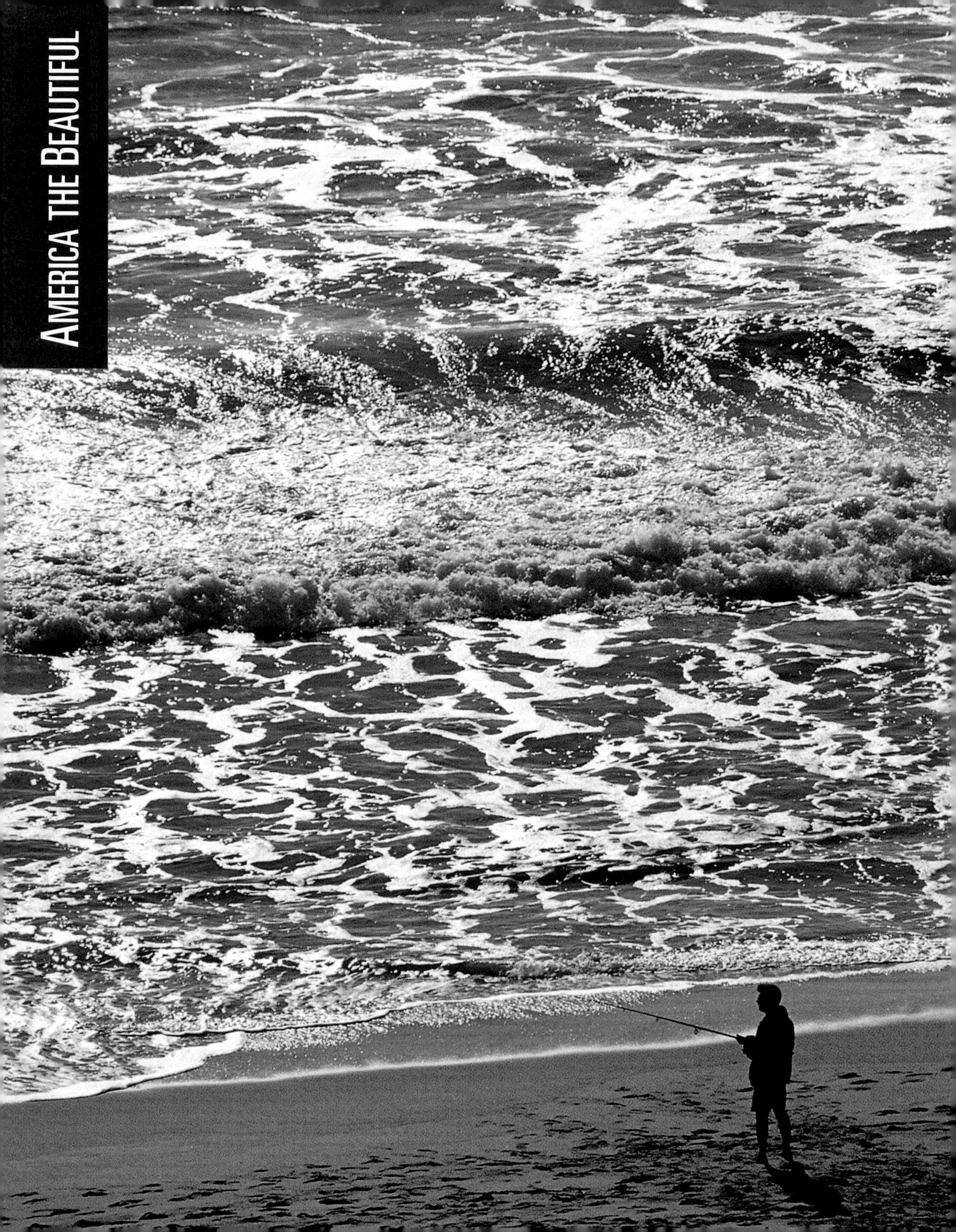

Delaware

Jean F. Blashfield

Children's Press®
A Division of Grolier Publishing
New York   London   Hong Kong   Sydney
Danbury, Connecticut

Frontispiece: Surf casting on the beach at Fenwick Island

Front cover: New Castle

Back cover: Henry Clay Mill

Consultant: Constance J. Cooper, Ph.D., Historical Society of Delaware

Please note: All statistics are as up-to-date as possible at the time of publication.

Visit Children's Press on the Internet at http://publishing.grolier.com

Book production by Editorial Directions, Inc.

Library of Congress Cataloging-in-Publication Data

Delaware / Jean F. Blashfield.
144 p. 24 cm.—(America the Beautiful. Second series)
Includes bibliographical references and index.
Summary : Describes the geography, plants, animals, history, economy, religions,
culture, sports, arts, and people of Delaware.
ISBN 0-516-21090-4
Delaware—Juvenile literature. [1.Delaware.] I. Title. II. Series.
F164.3.B57 2000
975.1—dc21   99-048164
                                                                                    CIP
                                                                                     AC

Acknowledgments

Like all writers, I am totally indebted to librarians. They are the people who treasure information, delight in organizing it, relish confirming it, and rejoice in sharing it. That indebtedness now extends also to state officials, who make certain that their websites are useful and accurate.

My special thanks go to the libraries of the East Coast during my sojourn in Virginia and Washington, D.C., as well as to the fine collections of the State Historical Society of Wisconsin.

Thank also to Patricia Maloney Markun, who always shared my joy discovering new places.

Rehoboth Beach

Great egrets

Port of Wilmington

Young Delawarean

Contents

Delaware Water Gap

Delaware Memorial Bridge

Young Delawareans at the beach

Ladybug

CHAPTER ONE

Big Names for a Small State

Legend says that Thomas Jefferson once compared Delaware to a diamond—small but with great value. Delaware's inborn value has not changed in more than 200 years. It is located at the heart of the East Coast and is able to spread its rays in almost any direction. Its traditions and long history of moderation encourage other states to listen when it expresses an opinion. Delaware is often called the Diamond State because of Thomas Jefferson's observation.

Delaware is situated near the center of the East Coast.

The Colony That Didn't Exist

If you read the story of colonial days written at the time, you won't find anything about the Delaware colony. It didn't exist. It was called New Sweden when the Swedes tried to settle it and New Amstel when the Dutch took over. Then, in 1683, when William Penn was granted land that became Pennsylvania, three

Opposite: Cypress trees at Trussem Pond

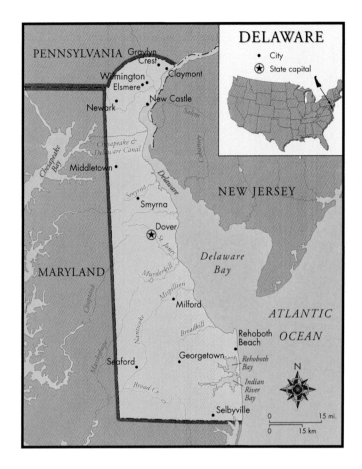

DELAWARE

- City
- ★ State capital

PENNSYLVANIA

Graylyn Crest
Wilmington
Elsmere
Claymont
New Castle
Newark
Chesapeake & Delaware Canal
Chesapeake Bay
Middletown
Smyrna
Dover
Delaware Bay
MARYLAND
Murderkill
Milford
Broadkill
Rehoboth Beach
Rehoboth Bay
Georgetown
Seaford
Indian River Bay
Broad Cr.
Selbyville

NEW JERSEY

ATLANTIC OCEAN

N

0   15 mi.

0   15 km

Geopolitical map of Delaware

little counties that ran along Delaware Bay were tossed in too so that Penn would have some seacoast. The three counties were usually referred to as the Lower Counties and then ignored.

But the residents of Delaware quietly went about their business of becoming very important to neighboring Philadelphia while gradually taking back the right to govern themselves. When independence from Britain was declared, Delaware declared its independence from Pennsylvania too. At that time, the Lower Colonies on the Delaware River settled on their permanent name—Delaware State.

Getting a Name

Delaware Bay got its name when a ship from the Virginia colony explored a wide bay early in the 1600s. The ship's captain, Samuel Argall, had to put something on the map he was making, so he named the bay after one of the founders of his own colony, Lord De La Warr. The name was modified to "Delaware" and given to the river that feeds into the bay, then to the Native Americans who lived around the bay, and eventually, to the state.

The First State

Delaware's people wanted to make certain that outsiders could never again take away their independence. They knew that, as small as they were, it was important that they be part of a strong nation. Thus, when the U.S. Constitution was written, they quickly prepared to study the important document.

Thirty delegates from throughout the new state met in Dover, reviewed what they saw, and signed the document on December 7, 1787—becoming the first state to do so. That swift action made this second-smallest state the first state in the new United States of America. Ever since, December 7 has been celebrated as Delaware Day and Delaware has been known as the First State.

Usually, being the First State has granted people from Delaware the right to enter first on national ceremonial occasions. In 1999, however, Delaware became a new "first" when the federal government issued the first of the new twenty-five-cent coins. Congressman Michael Castle of Delaware originally proposed the new coins. Eventually, each state will have a quarter, with a design representing the state on one side and George Washington on the other, or "heads," side.

The "tails" side of the first coin shows Delaware hero Caesar Rodney galloping from Dover to Philadelphia to cast his vote for the Declaration of Independence. This image was chosen in a statewide poll.

The 1999 Delaware quarters feature Caesar Rodney.

Other Nicknames

Most people in the United States know Delaware as the First State, but Delawareans are equally proud of another nickname—the Blue Hen State. Soldiers from Delaware, going to fight the red-coated British soldiers, carried with them a breed of blue roosters that they had found to be successful in the bloody but popular sport of cockfighting. Delaware's blue hens were feisty and determined. So were Delaware's soldiers. They proudly carried the nickname Blue Hens Chickens into battle.

Delaware's beaches are popular with Delawareans and tourists.

Small wonder, then, that Delaware is proud of its nicknames. The people of Delaware may not go in for cockfighting anymore—in fact, that sport is illegal—but they know that, despite its size, Delaware is indeed a wondrous place. Its beaches are among the most popular on the Atlantic Coast. Its businesses—headed by the gigantic chemical firm of DuPont—have made the state among the most prosperous in America. Its contributions to the history and culture of the United States are unchallenged. Small wonder, then, that Delaware's newest nickname is the Small Wonder.

CHAPTER TWO

Colonial Delaware

Humans had lived along this eastern river and bay for probably thousands of years before Europeans arrived in the region. Europeans found a native people who called themselves Lenape (LEN-uh-pay, meaning "First People" or "People Who are the Standard"). The English later called them the Delaware, after the river and the bay where they lived.

The Lenape (sometimes called Lenni-Lenape) are Algonquin-speaking American Indians, though different groups spoke different dialects. They had apparently lived along the river for many centuries and had established permanent farmlands. Although they lived in many different communities, they were divided into only three clans—the Munsee (Wolf), the Unalachtigo (Turkey), and the Unami (Turtle). The men hunted and the women farmed. They taught the first colonists, who came from Sweden, to grow corn. In 1748, the Lenape dug up the skeletons of their chiefs and moved from Delaware to the western part of Pennsylvania.

Europeans also found a people called the Minqua or Susquehannock in the Delaware area. They were related to the Iroquois of what is now upper New York. They had been in the region for some time, trying to take over the land of the Lenape. A smaller Algonquin tribe called the Nanticoke (Tidewater People) lived in the far southern section.

Hundreds of years ago, the Lenape made their home in what is now Delaware.

Opposite: Early life along the Delaware River

Italian explorer
John Cabot

Early Explorers

When the English heard about Christopher Columbus's discoveries in the Caribbean, they, too, wanted new worlds to claim as their own. King Henry VII, in 1496, authorized Italian-born navigator Giovanni Caboto (who had moved to England and changed his name to John Cabot) to explore in the king's name. On June 24, 1497, Cabot claimed the continent for England, ignoring the obvious signs of human life at the place he landed, probably in Canada.

Henry Hudson, exploring for the Netherlands, sailed into Delaware Bay in 1609. Because he found it difficult to navigate the many shoals, or sand bars, in the bay, he did not go far up river. Instead, he explored a river farther north that soon took his name. This exploration gave the Dutch a claim to the lands around these two rivers.

The Dutch West India Company built their main settlement on Manhattan Island at the mouth of the Hudson River, but their captains continued to explore the Delaware River, using lighter and smaller boats that would not get stuck on the shoals. They quickly discovered the abundant wildlife that made the area attractive.

The First Settlement

Dutch merchants created the first European settlement in Delaware in early 1631. Led by Samuel Godyn, they bought land on a river later called Lewes Creek. Thirty-two settlers built a large house within a big fenced area and called their community Zwaanendael (Valley of the Swans).

When the merchants' ship returned the following year, the men had disappeared. It was Delaware's only Indian massacre and it occurred because one Indian became so fascinated by a shiny metal coat of arms that he stole it. His own tribe killed him because he had gone against their rules of peace, and the dead man's friends took revenge against the Dutch.

New Sweden

Sweden soon began to eye the land on Delaware Bay. At that time, a chancellor ruled Sweden in the name of the child queen, Christina. He hoped to establish a colony that could provide an income for Sweden by growing tobacco and collecting fur pelts for sale in Europe. He hired Peter Minuit, who had been a leader of the Dutch West India Company and governor of Dutch-controlled New Amsterdam in New York, until he lost that position as a result of political intrigue.

In March 1638, Peter Minuit's two ships, the *Kalmar Nyckel* and the *Fogel Grip,* dropped anchor at the mouth of the river called Minquas Kill, where Wilmington stands today. Minuit built Fort Christina on high ground nearby.

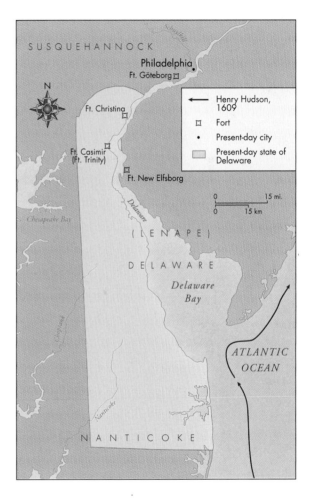

Exploration of Delaware

The End of Peter Minuit

Peter Minuit, the leader of the New Sweden expedition, planned to return to Sweden by way of the West Indies. While in harbor at St. Christopher, he boarded a Dutch ship. A hurricane suddenly struck, and all ships quickly sailed out into the sea, where they could handle the high winds better than in a small harbor. But the Dutch ship with Minuit aboard sank in the storm and the *Kalmar Nyckel* returned to Sweden without the colony's leader. ■

Five chiefs of the Lenape tribes agreed to sell 67 miles (108 kilometers) along the river, from Bombay Hook to the Schuylkill River, where Philadelphia is today. However, as often happened in early American history, the Native Americans and the would-be settlers had very different ideas about the agreement.

New Sweden's settlers, who included both Swedes and Finns, came ashore and immediately started planting tobacco. They also traded directly with the Minqua for fur pelts. They filled their ship with beaver and bear furs and took these treasures back to Sweden. The *Fogel Grip* was sent down to Virginia to trade for tobacco. The English refused to trade, but the ship returned with an African-American man called Antonius or Black Anthony. He was apparently an indentured servant, not a slave. An indentured servant is someone who agrees to work without pay for a period of time in exchange for passage on a ship.

The settlement was left with twenty-six men, living in one large log cabin. They planted some crops, including corn, as the Lenape had taught them, and they traded for furs. The *Kalmar Nyckel* returned to New Sweden two years later, in April 1640. On board was a clergyman—the first Lutheran minister in America.

New Sweden never had a central village. All the colonists lived on isolated farms, but they could get together when they wanted. The homes they built—America's first log cabins—were typical of the houses built in the forests of Scandinavia. Swedish settlers lived as far up the Delaware River as the site of what is now Philadelphia. They called the river New Swedeland Stream.

In 1641, Englishmen from Connecticut came into New Sweden and—completely ignoring the Swedes—built a settlement south of

Fort Christina. When the Swedes protested, the English just pulled up the boundary stake and sent it to them in response.

The following May, a ship arrived carrying a new governor, Johan Printz, a man with considerable military experience. Printz built two forts: New Elfsborg, to take control of the river, and Fort Göteborg, near present-day Chester, to watch the Indians. These forts angered both Dutch and English traders, who were used to free trade in the area.

Sweden's Johan Printz hindered trading along the Delaware River.

Peter Stuyvesant

Dutch Land Grabbing

Back in Europe, the Dutch and Swedes were on good terms with each other, so their settlers in America were expected to get along well too. But Peter Stuyvesant of New Amsterdam (later New York) wanted to take the Delaware region and its trade away from the Swedes. He sent a fleet of eleven ships sailing up and down the Delaware River, blasting their cannons, but not actually attacking the Swedish settlements.

Stuyvesant made an agreement with two Indian chiefs that the Dutch would have the right to the land on the western side of the Delaware River from Minquas Kill to the coast. But the Indians did not actually sell the

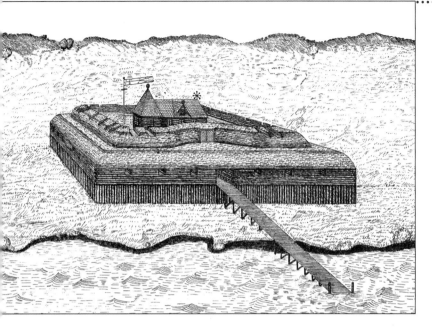

Fort Casimir was built on the current site of New Castle.

land. Stuyvesant built Fort Casimir where New Castle is now located.

Both the Dutch colony of New Amsterdam and the Swedish colony of New Sweden were quite small and poorly armed. Their squabbling about who owned the Delaware River was more like two villages fighting than two European powers at war. But they were very different in the way they treated the Native Americans. The Dutch tended to take what they wanted and kill Indians who got in the way while the Swedes had strict orders to treat the native people kindly.

Printz collected proof from the Indians that they had sold the land to the Swedes, but when he sent the proof to Stuyvesant, the Dutch leader ignored it. Gradually, month by month, Stuyvesant took control of the river.

Back and Forth

In 1654, a ship carrying new immigrants and a new governor, Johan Rising, sailed for New Sweden. After a terrible journey complicated by pirates, Europe's Thirty Years' War, and contagious disease, the ship finally arrived in New Sweden. It had been six years since Sweden had sent a ship. Its arrival increased New Sweden's population to well more than 300 people.

The new governor, discovering the Dutch only lightly defended Fort Casimir, demanded the Dutch surrender—and they did. The few soldiers and some Dutch farmers living nearby agreed. A jubilant Governor Rising renamed the fort—Fort Trinity.

Johan Rising had great dreams for New Sweden, and during the winter of 1654 and spring of 1655, he set about making them happen. But while he was concentrating on expanding farm and establishing churches, Peter Stuyvesant was preparing to attack. Soon a shipload of soldiers arrived from old Amsterdam—more troops than there were people in New Sweden.

On August 31, 1655, the Dutch soldiers demanded the surrender of Fort Trinity. The Swedish soldiers, overwhelmed, agreed, after one Swede was killed—by his own side. And Fort Trinity became Fort Casimir again.

Only thirty Swedish farmers manned Fort Christina, the area's first fort, but they managed to hold off the much larger Dutch

The Battle That Never Was

Nineteenth-century writer Washington Irving (right), used the pen name Diedrich Knickerbocker. He made fun of the Dutch expedition in his *History of New York from the Beginning of the World to the End of the Dutch Dynasty*.

Although Fort Trinity actually surrendered without a fight, Irving described a battle: "Bang! went the guns; whack! went the broadswords; thump! went the cudgels; crash! went the musket-stocks; blows, kicks, cuffs, scratches, black eyes and bloody noses swelling the horrors of the scene! Thick, thwack, cut and hawk, helter-skelter, higgledy-piggledy, hurly-burly, heads-over-heels, rough-and-tumble! Dunder and blixum! swore the Dutchmen; splitter and splutter! cried the Swedes." ■

force for two weeks. While the siege went on, the Dutch destroyed the farms and houses of the Swedish settlers. On September 15, 1655, Johan Rising surrendered. Many Swedes stayed in Delaware, agreeing to become Dutch subjects.

Thus ended the short-lived colony of New Sweden. It would be almost 200 years before more Swedish immigrants arrived in America. Eventually, though, more than 1 million Swedes would come to the United States.

For a while, the city of Amsterdam in the Netherlands owned a portion of Delaware south of the Christina River. The merchants there changed the name of Fort Casimir to New Amstel, and it eventually became New Castle. They prepared to help it prosper, especially by buying tobacco in Maryland for sale in Europe. But they hadn't counted on the English.

The Coming of the English

Back in Europe, the English and the Dutch had emerged from the Thirty Years' War as friendly enemies—politically allies but commercially at war. In 1664, an English squadron sailed up the Hudson River and forced Peter Stuyvesant to surrender New Amsterdam. The colony was then given to the English king's brother, the duke of York, and it became New York.

New Amstel also became the property of the duke of York. He pretty much left the colonists alone except in terms of government. Knowing that he would someday be the king of England, he set about ruling the colony with a firm hand—as if to get in practice. The few people who rebelled were tried for treason. One of them, Marcus Jacobson, was shipped to Barbados in the Caribbean as a

The surrender of
New Amsterdam
to the English

slave. That ended any idea of further rebellion during the eighteen years that the duke of York controlled Delaware.

During this period, the Dutch gave up all claim to lands in North America in exchange for Suriname (formerly Dutch Guiana) in South America. Also, the English divided Delaware into three court districts, which later became counties.

Historical map
of Delaware

William Penn

The son of an English admiral, William Penn leaned toward becoming a Quaker while attending Oxford University in England. The Quaker faith called for direct communion with God. It also eliminated the elaborate church hierarchy that existed in the Church of England. The Quaker faith—officially called the Society of

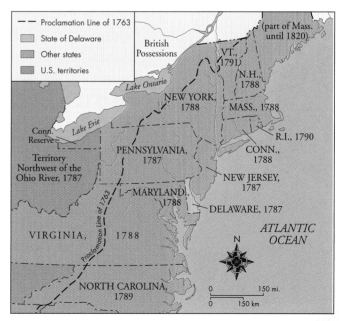

William Penn controlled
Pennsylvania and
Delaware for many
years.

Friends—was outlawed at that time. Penn gradually became a devout Quaker and even went to prison twice for spreading his beliefs.

The English crown owed Admiral Penn a great deal of money. When the admiral died, his son William agreed to take payment in land in North America extending west from the Delaware River. Penn regarded the colony he planned to start there as a "holy experiment," a place where religious refugees would be welcome.

Penn was disappointed not to have access to the sea from his colony, however. He requested that the duke of York also give him the three counties along the Delaware River, and the duke agreed. For the next ninety years, colonial Delaware was attached to Pennsylvania as the Lower Counties.

William Penn's charter made him the owner of the colony. He had the right to collect the earnings of the colony and to establish its government. When Penn and several other owners of smaller colonies began to let the people create their own governments, the king of England became alarmed. Few proprietary colonies were given after 1690.

Wanting to Be Delaware

During the following years, Lord Baltimore of Maryland kept trying to expand his colony into Delaware. It took a number of decisions—the last made in 1750—for Delaware's boundaries to be settled.

William Penn left Pennsylvania in 1684 and did not return for fifteen years. For two years in the 1690s, Pennsylvania was taken away from William Penn by the new English monarchs, William and Mary. The colony was placed under the rule of Governor Benjamin Fletcher of New York, who was thoroughly disliked.

The Lower Counties took advantage of the situation to carry out a small rebellion. They pulled their representatives out of Pennsylvania's governing council, which continually favored the Quakers. Pennsylvanians didn't object because now they had more say in the council than they had when Delaware's representatives were included.

From London, Penn appointed a separate governor for Delaware—his cousin, William Markham. Delawareans were happy to have Markham as their governor because he knew the land and the people. When Penn's right to the colony was reinstated in 1694, Penn named Markham governor of both Pennsylvania and the Lower Counties.

Penn gave in to the continuing complaints of the Delawareans and, in 1701, granted the Lower Counties their own charter and legislature, which first met in 1704. Now, instead of two governors and one assembly, there were two assemblies but only one governor.

The English government started to make moves to turn all American colonies into Crown colonies, a change that would take away Penn's rights. Penn hurried to England once again and never returned. Penn's right to his colony was confirmed, though, and when he died in 1718, his widow, Hannah, became the proprietor of Pennsylvania. After her death in 1727, each son became proprietor in succession, but they played little part in the life of the

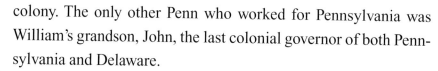

John Penn

colony. The only other Penn who worked for Pennsylvania was William's grandson, John, the last colonial governor of both Pennsylvania and Delaware.

The Coming of Revolution

During the following decades, Delaware pretty much went its own way. The assembly—to which men were elected for a year at a time—was supposed to submit any laws it passed to either Penn or the Crown for approval. In reality, no one paid much attention to what Delaware did. Pennsylvania, on the other hand, had to have everything approved. Whenever the assembly in Pennsylvania tried to influence Delaware, residents of the Lower Counties proudly insisted that they were independent of their larger neighbor.

During the 1760s and 1770s, the British Parliament passed many laws. Many of these laws confirmed the colonists' growing suspicion that the British cared only about taking money from the colonies and keeping them under control. People in America began to say that the colonies should control their own destinies.

Pirates in the Bay

Throughout the colonial years, the East Coast's bays and inlets often served as hideouts for pirates who roamed the seas hunting for treasure among the many ships crossing the Atlantic. Delaware Bay was one of their hiding places. Because the eastern side of the bay has a dangerous seabed, it's likely that if treasure were ever buried along the bay's shores, it was in Delaware. Edward Teach (left)—better known as Blackbeard—and Captain Kidd are among the notorious pirates who, according to legend, may have found the shores of Delaware a good place to hide their treasure. ■

"Penman of the Revolution"

A Quaker lawyer who had trained in London, John Dickinson (right) always looked for a middle ground in arguments. Unfortunately, the coming American Revolution did not allow a middle ground. Although he was not eager to separate from the mother country, Dickinson felt that the colonies should be united in their decision to rebel against certain laws.

When the possibility of declaring independence was introduced at the Continental Congress in 1776, John Adams spoke in favor and Dickinson spoke against. Dickinson still hoped that England and the colonies could resolve their differences. However, once independence was declared and the battle won, Dickinson did all he could to help the new nation get off on the right foot. He helped to write both the Articles of Confederation and the U.S. Constitution. ■

The Quakers who controlled Pennsylvania became increasingly reluctant to make any moves that would indicate to Parliament that they didn't trust the mother country. Delawareans, on the other hand, were just as glad to have the Crown ignore them. John Dickinson, a Philadelphia lawyer who had a farm near Dover, began to write thoughtful essays called "Letters from a Farmer in Pennsylvania," which appeared in colonial newspapers. They helped turn public opinion against some of the measures that England was taking against its colonies.

Prosperity

Early in their history, the American colonies tended to divide along northern and southern lines. The Middle Colonies, which lay in between—Delaware, New York, New Jersey, and Pennsylvania— served as a middle ground in ideas. Maryland, although it almost surrounds Delaware, was regarded as a southern colony.

As the American Revolution approached, New York and Pennsylvania joined their interests to build large American and international markets. They became the most prosperous of the colonies. Delaware was tied to Pennsylvania, and New Jersey was tied to New York.

The Middle Colonies were sometimes called the Flour Colonies because their principal crop was wheat. Partly because they were so prosperous, the Middle Colonies had few objections to the way Britain treated the colonies.

Separation from Britain

On June 29, 1774, 500 citizens met at the New Castle Court House and voted to support Boston merchants in shutting down trade with Britain. They also called for a special assembly of the colonies to make joint decisions. Caesar Rodney, Thomas McKean, and George Read represented Delaware in the First Continental Congress in 1774 and again in the Second Continental Congress in 1775. The 1775 Congress voted to raise a colonial army if it should become necessary. It was necessary—the war had already begun in Massachusetts.

Meeting in June 1776, the Continental Congress first called for each colony to form a new government that would not reflect its old colonial status. Delaware was one of the first colonies to do so. On June 15, the Delaware assembly voted itself out of existence as a representative of the British crown, and then voted itself back into existence as representatives of the people.

In the Lower Counties, a constitutional convention met in August. Under the leadership of George Read of New Castle, it created a constitution for the new state, with no mention of Pennsylvania.

A New Name

A new state deserved a new name. The region along the lower Delaware River had long been referred to by such names as the Lower Counties, the Delaware River Counties, or even the long and awkward Counties of New Castle, Kent, and Sussex upon Delaware. One of the first things the convention did was vote to call their region Delaware State. ■

As representatives of Delaware State, Rodney, McKean, and Read attended the Continental Congress meetings in Philadelphia that hot summer of 1776. Each colony had only one vote, regardless of the number of men in its delegation. The three men had to reach a majority opinion in order to cast Delaware's vote. It was an important vote—nothing more or less than independence from Britain.

Thomas McKean supported the Declaration of Independence.

A statue of Caesar Rodney commemorating his famous ride

When it came time to discuss Richard Henry Lee's motion for independence on July 1, Rodney was away, attending to his military duties. McKean planned to vote for the Declaration of Independence. Read planned to vote against it (though he later signed it). They needed Rodney's vote to break their tie.

Caesar Rodney—sick and worn-out—rode 80 miles (129 km) through a stormy night from Kent County to Philadelphia. Exhausted, he arrived in time to cast his vote in favor of the declaration. Delaware's vote for independence allowed the thirteen "states" to present a united front to Britain. Rodney's ride took its place in American legend along with the midnight ride of Paul Revere in Massachusetts.

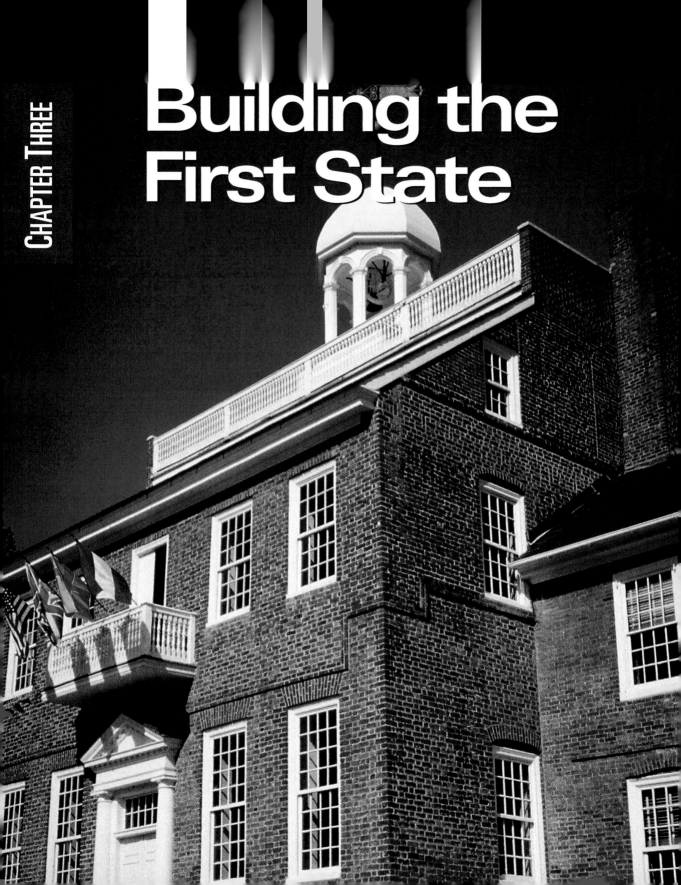

CHAPTER THREE

Building the First State

The legislature of Delaware chose John McKinly, a revolution-minded physician from Wilmington, as the state's president. The real power, though, rested in a four-man group called the Privy Council.

Delaware's first assembly was divided between conservatives, who were not too happy with the idea of independence, and revolutionaries, who were delighted. It was the job of the leaders, such as John Dickinson and George Read, to get these two sides to work together.

Wartime

In the early days of the Revolutionary War, British general William Howe decided to approach Philadelphia, the colonies' largest city, via Chesapeake Bay instead of Delaware Bay. The mouth of the Delaware River was too well protected by American troops. The British army headed overland, with George Washington's troops fighting them every mile.

Eight days later, the largest fight of Howe's trek toward Philadelphia took place in the Battle of the Brandywine, across the border in Pennsylvania. Howe's redcoats surprised the American soldiers and forced them to retreat. Troops then captured the town of Wilmington—along with all the new state's records and presi-

General William Howe of Great Britain

Opposite: New Castle's Old Court House was built in 1732.

The New Flag

The only Revolutionary War battle on Delaware soil was the Battle of Cooch's Bridge, near Newark, on September 3, 1777. According to tradition, the new American flag, bearing thirteen stars, was flown for the first time during this brief battle. ■

dent, John McKinly. With continual skirmishes on the Delaware River endangering New Castle, the capital of the state was moved south to Dover.

The British left Wilmington in October 1777 and Philadelphia in 1778. The regiments of soldiers sent from Delaware continued to fight as the action moved southward toward Virginia. The war finally ended in 1783, and Americans were free to concentrate on building a new nation.

A Failed Government

While the Declaration of Independence was being written, the representatives at the Continental Congress also wrote an agreement called the Articles of Confederation. It bound the states together loosely because many of the representatives did not want a strong central government. Delaware was the second to last state to agree to—or ratify—the articles.

The major problem with the Articles of Confederation was that it gave the government no power to tax the states, so the government had no funds. Nor could it control trade among the states. Delaware was one of the first to see that the system didn't work and to call for amending the articles. But the states could not agree on how to fix the problems.

In 1786, representatives from each state were asked to gather in Annapolis, Maryland, to discuss changes in the articles. Only five states, including Delaware, sent representatives. The following year, another attempt was made, and they met in Philadelphia. The session was called the Constitutional Convention, and this time it succeeded.

George Washington presiding at the Constitutional Convention in 1787

Forming a New Government

George Read, one of Delaware's five representatives, was instructed by Delaware's general assembly to make sure that Delaware—despite its small size—had a vote equal to other states. This insistence resulted in the formation of the Senate, in which each state had an equal voice. The other, larger states were equally determined to have a legislative body in which each state had a number of representatives in proportion to its population. This demand produced the House of Representatives.

Part of the decision making involved the capital of the United States. Philadelphia, as the largest city, had long been regarded as the capital. But it was a distinctly northern city. In a compromise, it was decided to build a completely new capital in a southern location, at the mouth of the Potomac River, between Virginia and Maryland.

Delaware became the first state by being the first to ratify the new Constitution of the United States of America. It then pro-

George Read

ceeded to write its own new constitution in 1791. The state constitutional convention did away with the Privy Council and reinstated the powerful position of governor. They also revised the court system. Most important, they decided that any free white man who paid taxes could vote. In the past, men had to own property in order to vote. The new state constitution also guaranteed freedom of religion.

Founding the Methodist Church

In England, John Wesley, joined by his brother Charles, had decided that the Church of England was too worldly, that believers had to have a "method" to their spiritual lives. They and their followers came to be called Methodists. In 1739, the Wesleys sent George Whitefield, a preacher friend, to preach in Delaware. Whitefield found enthusiastic listeners in Delaware, where religious diversity had long been accepted. He developed a small congregation at Lewes.

Thirty years later, the Wesleys sent many more missionaries to the American colonies and congregations began to grow. One missionary, Francis Asbury, unlike the others, remained in the colonies during the Revolution. He helped the Americans, especially in Delaware, to establish circuit riders. These circuit riders were preachers who moved from church to church on a regular schedule, preaching and encouraging the growth of faith.

Barratt's Chapel, near Frederica, was built by a well-to-do farmer. It often drew crowds when preachers spoke there. In 1784, Francis Asbury met John Wesley's representative, Thomas Coke, at Barratt's Chapel. The two agreed that it was time to organize a new

John Wesley left the Church of England and helped create the Methodist denomination.

George Whitefield preaching to a group in Delaware

church, which they called the Methodist Episcopal Church. They declared the new church's independence from the Church of England, though the Wesleys in England had not yet broken away. Barratt's Chapel has since been known as the "cradle of American Methodism." Methodism soon became the largest faith in nineteenth-century Delaware.

The du Ponts

Pierre Samuel du Pont de Nemours was a French nobleman who had been King Louis XVI's minister of finance. One of his sons, Eleuthère-Irénée, was a friend of Antoine Lavoisier, later known as the founder of modern chemistry. When Lavoisier was beheaded during the French Revolution, the du Ponts decided to leave France.

The family arrived on the East Coast on New Year's Day, 1800, ready to start a new century in a new land. At first, they planned to start a business-oriented colony in Virginia that would tempt

Eleuthère-Irénée du Pont

Frenchmen to immigrate. When they could not get enough money for that, Irénée looked elsewhere.

The du Ponts quickly discovered that American-made gunpowder was of very poor quality. Using his father's chemical knowledge, Eleuthère-Irénée, or Irénée, built a gunpowder factory on Brandywine Creek in northern Delaware.

The first gunpowder went on sale in 1802. Irénée had become friends with Virginian Thomas Jefferson, who arranged for the DuPont factory to be given government contracts for their gunpowder. Its greatly improved quality was proved in the War of 1812.

In 1818, the DuPont gunpowder factory exploded, killing forty men. In a move that was very unusual for the time, Irénée gave pensions to the widows and saw that the children of the dead workers were educated.

Before the end of the nineteenth century, the du Pont family was the wealthiest family in Delaware. At the start of the twenty-first century, the firm of E. I. du Pont de Nemours remains the

The War of 1812

The United States had barely begun to function as a nation when it was forced to go to war with Britain in what came to be called the War of 1812. (The war lasted into 1815.) British ships tried to bombard Delaware from the bay.

In March 1813, a British squadron threatened to destroy the city of Lewes. An army of 1,000 men gathered and prevented the British ships from landing troops on Delaware soil.

A house in Lewes is known as Cannonball House because it was struck by a cannonball during a two-day British bombardment in April 1813. The cannonball still remains in the house. ∎

largest chemical research firm in the world. (For many years, the du Ponts themselves disagreed on whether "Du" should be capitalized. In this book, we refer to the people as "du Pont" and the company as "DuPont.")

Making Travel Easier

Businessmen of Delaware saw the success the Erie Canal in New York was having and decided in 1824 to build a canal connecting Chesapeake Bay and the Delaware River. The Chesapeake and Delaware Canal cut almost 300 miles

A bridge over the Chesapeake and Delaware Canal

(483 km) off the journey from Baltimore to Philadelphia. It runs from the Elk River off northern Chesapeake Bay almost straight eastward through New Castle County to Reedy Point on the Delaware River. It became an immediate success when it opened in 1829, despite the high cost.

Originally, the 19-mile (31-km) canal had a series of locks to handle the slight change in elevation between the two ends. In 1919, the U.S. government bought the canal, which has since been run by the U.S. Army corps of engineers. They widened it and changed it to one level so that the locks could be removed. It is still one of the busiest canals in the world, though much of the traffic today is private pleasure boats. The canal has been widened to about 450 feet (137 meters) to accommodate large ships. Several bridges cross the canal, including a new and beautiful suspension bridge at St. George's.

A rail line was built by the New Castle and Frenchtown Railroad in 1831. At first, the cars were pulled by horses, but within months a steam engine called the Delaware was brought from Britain and the nation's first scheduled passenger-carrying steam railroad began service. (The Baltimore and Ohio, which began service in 1827, was a freight line.) By 1838, Philadelphia and Wilmington were linked by rail.

Steam and Oliver Evans

In 1790, Newport native Oliver Evans obtained the first patent on a steam engine in the United States. Fifteen years later, he made a steam engine that was even more powerful than the one invented by James Watt in Scotland. He ran a dredge and, to get it to where it was needed, he put wheels on it, thus making the first steam-powered vehicle (above). Evans did not live to see the first steam railroad in Delaware in service in 1832. It ran from New Castle to Frenchtown. Evans also invented an automated flour mill, which helped Delaware farmers. ∎

The Question of Slavery

In Delaware, as elsewhere in the North, the first half of the nineteenth century was a combination of learning to be a part of the United States and dealing with growing sentiments against slavery. Delaware reflected the United States as a whole. The northern section, which rejected slavery, was oriented toward industrial Philadelphia. The southern part, largely rural, favored slavery because it held southern attitudes, even though its agriculture did not require hundreds of workers.

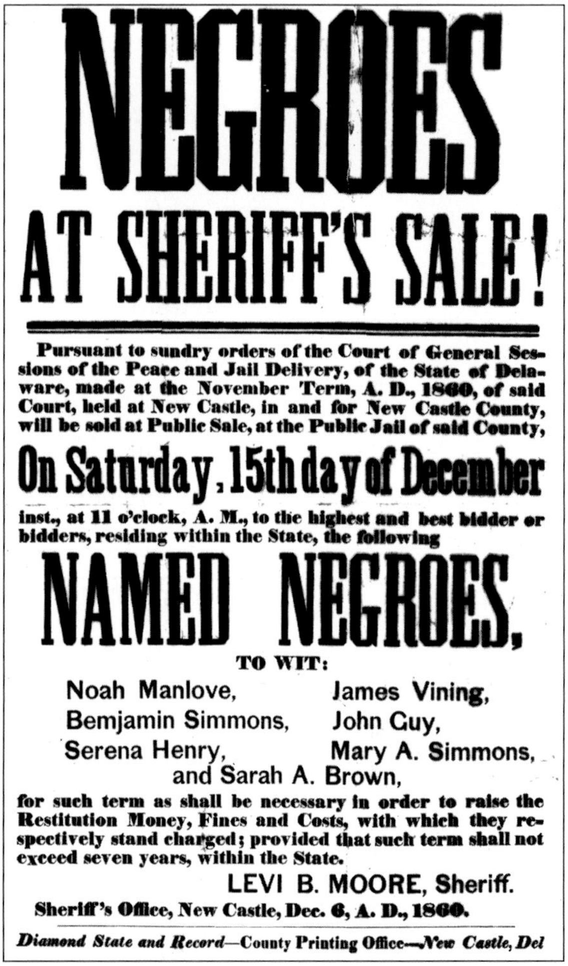

Delaware had an additional factor—the large number of Quakers who had settled in the state. Quakers in general were opposed to slavery and most of the leading abolitionists of the day were Quakers.

The Delaware legislature had outlawed the sale of slaves across state lines. However, some Delawareans saw people in other states making money by selling their slaves, and they began to smuggle their slaves out of the state. A large business in smuggling and selling slaves existed in Sussex County for some years.

At the same time, other people were smuggling runaway slaves through Delaware and helping them escape to freedom in the North. The organized route by which slaves could reach Canada was called the Underground Railroad. It had several stops in

NEGROES
AT SHERIFF'S SALE!

Pursuant to sundry orders of the Court of General Sessions of the Peace and Jail Delivery, of the State of Delaware, made at the November Term, A. D., 1860, of said Court, held at New Castle, in and for New Castle County, will be sold at Public Sale, at the Public Jail of said County,

On Saturday, 15th day of December

inst., at 11 o'clock, A. M., to the highest and best bidder or bidders, residing within the State, the following

NAMED NEGROES,

TO WIT:

Noah Manlove,   James Vining,
Bemjamin Simmons,   John Guy,
Serena Henry,   Mary A. Simmons,
          and Sarah A. Brown,

for such term as shall be necessary in order to raise the Restitution Money, Fines and Costs, with which they respectively stand charged; provided that such term shall not exceed seven years, within the State.

LEVI B. MOORE, Sheriff.

Sheriff's Office, New Castle, Dec. 6, A. D., 1860.

Diamond State and Record—County Printing Office—*New Castle, Del*

An 1860 advertisement for slaves

Delaware. One man, Thomas Garrett of Wilmington, helped more than 2,700 slaves to reach freedom in the north.

Just before the Civil War began, Delaware had fewer than 2,000 slaves. The state had close to 20,000 freed blacks in its population—more than any other state.

The Civil War

Delaware was considered a border state during the Civil War (1861–1865). Its people were divided on whether they supported the North or the South. However, Delaware was closer to northern in its sentiments than was surrounding Maryland. Most people wanted to preserve the Union, but didn't think the North had the right to attack the eleven states that had seceded and formed the Confederate States of America. However, Delaware stayed with the Union.

Henry du Pont headed the Delaware militia during the Civil War.

No battles were fought on Delaware soil, but Delaware willingly provided soldiers for the Civil War. At least 12,000 men served, though several companies were so pro-South that their weapons were taken away. At least half of the Union's gunpowder came from the DuPont powder mills.

Henry du Pont was put in charge of Delaware's militia. His cousin, Samuel Francis Du Pont (he spelled his name that way), was commander of the Philadelphia Navy Yard in 1860 and emerged from the war as a rear admiral. He was a leader in developing the Union's naval blockade strategy, which kept supplies from Europe from reaching the South. Wilmington, an important shipbuilding center, constructed a number of vessels—including ironclads, or armored ships—for the U.S. Navy.

The Terrible Prison

Fort Delaware, on Pea Patch Island in the Delaware River, was originally built during the War of 1812 to guard Philadelphia from attack by the British. It was rebuilt in the 1850s and was ready for use as a prison when the Civil War started. Damp and cold because of its location in the river, it had a fearful reputation.

After the Battle of Gettysburg in 1863, the prison-fort held at least 12,000 prisoners—more than twice as many as it was planned for. Diseases, especially smallpox, spread through the prison population. The prisoners all suffered from malnutrition, even though Delawareans who lived in the area sometimes tried to send in fresh fruits and vegetables.

Despite its terrible history, the fort became one of Delaware's first state parks in 1951. In the 1990s, the federal government contributed to its restoration. ■

Delaware's slaves, as elsewhere in the nation, were freed by the Thirteenth Amendment to the Constitution. That 1865 amendment confirmed President Abraham Lincoln's Emancipation Proclamation of 1863, which freed the slaves in the Confederate states.

Even after the war, Delawareans remained divided on how they felt about secession, Reconstruction (the military occupation of the states that had seceded), and the federal laws changing the rights of African-Americans. Congress passed the Fifteenth Amendment to the Constitution, guaranteeing the right to vote regardless of race. Enough states had ratified the amendment by 1870 for it to become law. Delaware, however, had no desire to give African-Americans the vote. It wasn't until 1901 that the General Assembly ratified that amendment, as a long-delayed formality—Tennessee didn't ratify it until 1997.

Some of the resentments left over from the Civil War affected Delaware for several decades. During this time, it was slow to give African-Americans any rights, education, or employment. In particular, the state did its best to keep African-Americans from voting. In some years, federal troops had to go to Delaware to make sure that elections were fair. But industry in Delaware was growing in importance, and old attitudes were starting to change.

Onto the Beaches

During these years, the Methodist Church remained the major denomination of Delaware, especially in Kent and Sussex Counties. It was the Methodists who started to turn Delaware's beautiful beaches into popular recreation areas.

In 1872, Reverend Robert W. Todd of Wilmington attended a camp meeting on the New Jersey shore. He came home so refreshed that he encouraged the Methodists to establish a similar Christian resort. They bought land on the shore at Rehoboth and laid out a campground, a collection of small cottages on the sand.

Members of the church gathered there for two-week periods every summer to enjoy the outdoors, each other's company, music, and church services.

Soon the Disciples of Christ from Pennsylvania opened up a resort on Bethany Beach. However, within ten years, as transportation improved, other people began coming to the beaches just for fun. In 1880, they held what may have been the nation's first beauty contest there. Individuals began buying land, and—despite the ever-present mosquitoes—the southern sands of Delaware turned the state into a vacation destination.

Rehoboth Beach was originally founded as a Christian resort.

CHAPTER FOUR

Twentieth-Century Delaware

The century began with Delawareans trying to figure the ins and outs of a new constitution. Though Democrats had long controlled many of the state's political offices, the Republicans were gradually taking over. This was primarily because the Democrats had refused, since the passage of the Fifteenth Amendment, to recognize African-American men as voters. They had also refused to give the heavily populated northern part of the state its due recognition.

DuPont's first headquarters at Eleutherian Mills

Much industry in northern Delaware changed during the early decades as a result of federal government lawsuit against the DuPont corporation. The firm, which was no longer a private family firm, had been buying up other gunpowder firms. The government decided that DuPont had established a monopoly that limited competition and broke it up. In 1912, DuPont sold off some of its gunpowder works to two new companies formed by employees and then started the search for other directions to go. DuPont then began its incredible growth.

The du Ponts were among the earliest automobile enthusiasts and helped to build Delaware's roads. T. Coleman du Pont paid for the nation's first divided highway, which eventually ran the length

Opposite: First USA Bank in Wilmington

of the state. Enthusiasm for cars also prompted the du Ponts to invest heavily in the fledgling General Motors (GM), making them the largest stockholders in that corporation, now the world's largest. Pierre du Pont became president of GM.

World War I

About 10,000 soldiers from Delaware served in the U.S. Army and Navy during World War I (1914–1918). The United States entered the war in 1917. The U.S. Army built a fort east of Milford to guard Delaware Bay. Named for a Delaware senator, Fort Saulsbury had four 12-inch (31-centimeter) guns pointing out into the mouth of the bay.

During World War I, a DuPont plant in Wilmington exploded, killing thirty-one people. Because DuPont was so deeply involved in chemical weapons, officials suspected that the plant had been sabotaged by enemy spies. Also during that war, German mines were found floating in Delaware Bay, though none exploded.

Many products from Delaware industries were important to the war effort so the state's economy boomed. In 1921, DuPont closed its 120-year-old powder yard, where the business had begun. (Many years later it was reopened as Hagley Museum.) The company expanded by buying up many other companies and their patents.

The economic growth of the state wasn't all industrial, nor was it all DuPont. Shipbuilding had been important to the state since before the Revolutionary War and remained so. The production of a soft leather called kid was also a major industry in Wilmington.

The poultry industry, which began in Delaware in the 1920s, brought great strength to the rural part of the state. The state's new highways allowed the farms of southern Delaware to find new and expanding markets. The highways also opened the beaches of southern Delaware to vacationers from the East.

The Education Revolution

During this period, Pierre S. du Pont began a revolution in Delaware's schools. There had never been any state supervision of the schools, little tax money was used to support them, and African-Americans were almost totally ignored. Delaware was the only state that refused to use tax money collected from white citizens to educate black children. A study in 1917 concluded, "Delaware buys a low and cheap brand of education."

In 1919, a new educational policy granted school taxes paid by white people to schools for African-Americans. Most schools for both races at that time were in pretty bad condition, and Pierre du Pont volunteered to build new schools. He even resigned his position as president of DuPont to take charge of the school-building program.

During the following years, most of the schools were rebuilt, mainly through the donation of du Pont's personal funds. He didn't just give money. He brought in experts to evaluate the state's schools and hired new administrators to

Pierre S. du Pont worked to improve Delaware schools.

follow the experts' advice. He created programs that helped schools stay within their budgets and yet function effectively and efficiently. Not everyone in the state agreed with du Pont and his changes. Many people resented his intrusion in matters that they regarded as their own business—even though they had neglected education for decades.

The Depression Years

Delaware's boom did not last long. The state joined the rest of the nation entering the Great Depression that began in 1929. Many people lost their jobs, and those who kept them often had large cuts in salary. The DuPont and related industries suffered a decline, but the state's poultry industry continued to grow throughout the depression.

Alfred I. du Pont led a fight to get old-age pensions for the people of Delaware before 1929. When the legislature voted down the idea, he developed his own list of people throughout the state who needed help and began to send them checks. Finally, in the 1930s, the state accepted the need for old-age pensions, and Delaware officials took over du Pont's growing list of people in need.

To survive during the depression, many people were put to work on projects paid for by the federal government. One of the main projects in Delaware carried out by the Civilian Conservation Corps (CCC) was mosquito control. Mosquitoes breed in wet areas, and they plagued the region near the marshes. The CCC dug ditches from the sea that allowed tides to flush through the marshes, eliminating mosquito larvae. In this way, mosquito pests were reduced greatly without the use of poisons.

Like Alfred I. du Pont and his cousin Pierre S. du Pont, major industrialists of Delaware helped pull the state through the depression. They organized the creation of parks and hospitals and encouraged school expansion.

In 1932, the Democratic Party of Delaware finally removed barriers against black voters. With the huge popularity of President Franklin D. Roosevelt, a Democrat elected that year with great African-American support, the state's Democrats also began to gain in popularity—though black voters were understandably reluctant to switch.

Alfred I. du Pont tried to help the less fortunate during the Great Depression.

A group from the Civilian Conservation Corps digging through marshland

World War II

World War II (1939–1945) brought a quick end to the depression. The war's emphasis on synthetics and other chemicals helped Delaware pull out of the economic slump more quickly than many states. Almost all that state's factories shifted their production to war work after the United States entered World War II in 1941. The state also reopened many shipyards, which had long been closed. One shipyard, Dravo in Wilmington, produced almost 200 ships during the war, including destroyer escort vessels.

DuPont played a major role in ending the war by managing the development of the Hanford Works in Washington State. The first atomic reactors were built there as part of the secret Manhattan Pro-

The Dravo shipyard produced many ships during World War II.

Bull Halsey

He was born in New Jersey and died in New York, but Admiral William "Bull" F. Halsey Jr. (right) regarded himself as a Delawarean. While he was elsewhere in the world during his naval career, all the women in his family, as well as his grandchildren, lived in Delaware. It was to Delaware that he came on leave.

When the United States entered World War II after Japan bombed Hawaii's Pearl Harbor, Halsey was in charge of the remaining U.S. Navy fleet in the Pacific. His men and his ships held off the Japanese while the United States rebuilt its fleet, and then proceeded to fight the Japanese on island after island. In October 1944, in the Battle of Leyte Gulf, Halsey's Third Fleet played a major role in the final destruction of the Japanese navy. ■

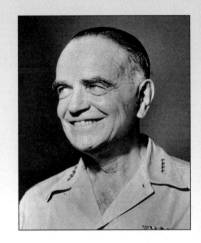

ject that produced the first atomic bomb. These reactors produced the element plutonium as part of their reaction. The plutonium was used in the atomic bombs that ended the war in the Pacific in 1945.

About one-tenth of the people in the state served in World War II. Other Delawareans guarded the ocean-front borders of their state in the event of attack. Fort DuPont at Delaware City and Fort Miles near Cape Henlopen were manned to guard the bay.

At Mid-Century

In 1951, the first Delaware Memorial Bridge opened, spanning the river between northern Delaware and New Jersey. For the first time, road traffic could head for New York without having to fight its way through Philadelphia or take a ferry across the bay to New Jersey. The 4.4-mile (7.1-km) Chesapeake Bay Bridge crossed the bay at Annapolis in 1952, making the beautiful beaches of Delaware accessible to Washingtonians.

Traveling along the East Coast got easier when the Delaware Memorial Bridge opened.

For several decades, African-Americans, not feeling very welcome in Delaware, had been moving away from the state. The state's population of African-Americans reached a low of 13.5 percent in 1940. During and after the war, the numbers of African-Americans again increased. However, in the 1950s, many whites began moving out of Wilmington into its suburbs. Wilmington was becoming a city of slums with a declining population.

At the same time, steps were being taken to integrate African-Americans more fully into the population of the state, especially in education. Northern Delaware was already integrating its high schools when the U.S. Supreme Court, in *Brown vs. Topeka Board of Education,* decided that the long-existing policy of "separate but equal" education was not constitutional. Two cases from Delaware were involved in that decision.

Educational changes alone, of course, did not solve Wilmington's problems. The wages paid to African-Americans were rarely anywhere near

During the 1950s, Wilmington suffered from poverty and a decreasing population.

those of white people. Yet African-Americans were the ones trying to keep the city going. In 1967, race riots broke out in the city, resulting in the arrests of 250 people. When rioting occurred again after the assassination of Reverend Martin Luther King Jr. the following year, Governor Charles L. Terry called in the National Guard to patrol the streets.

But when Governor Terry didn't send the troops away after things calmed down, the anger simmered. It wasn't until January 1969 that a new governor, Russell Peterson, called off the National Guard. Fair-housing laws were passed that made it illegal to discriminate against black people in renting or selling homes.

One of the programs started soon after that was meant to help revitalize the inner city of Wilmington. For the first time in U.S. history, a city, under Mayor Thomas Maloney, offered abandoned houses to anybody who wanted them to homestead. In the early days of the United States, newly opened lands were homesteaded, meaning that if people lived on the land and farmed it, the land became theirs.

In Wilmington, if people lived in the rundown houses as they fixed them up, they could buy them for as little as one dollar. Gradually, young people who could not have afforded nice homes any other way homesteaded many houses in the slums and helped improve Wilmington's future.

Chemistry has been vital to business in Delaware, but some things are even more important. About 1970, Shell Oil tried to build a refinery along the shore. It had already become clear that the waters of Delaware Bay and the river were polluted, so the state passed the Coastal Zone Act, which outlawed all chemical plants along the coast. This act became a signal to many other states and the federal government to protect the fragile seacoasts.

In the 1970s, Delaware had the highest tax rate in the country.

Governor Pete du Pont made changes that improved Delaware's economy.

When Pierre du Pont IV, called Pete, was elected governor in 1977, he decided it was time to cure the state's economic problems. First, he cut spending and balanced the budget. Then he gathered all the important government officials and businesspeople together. They decided that it was time to change the state's banking and corporation laws. Their decisions have brought a huge number of companies to Delaware, greatly improving the state's economic picture.

Dover AFB and Giant Airplanes

The only major military base in Delaware is the airport for military people and cargo between the United States and Europe and the Middle East. Dover Air Force Base was opened during World War II when Dover Municipal Airport was turned into a base to train fighter pilots. Today, this huge airfield is the home base of the air mobility command and the C-5 Galaxy, the largest cargo plane ever built. It's been said that an eight-lane bowling alley could fit inside one of the planes. ■

End of the Century

An important voice in the U.S. Senate since 1973 has been Delaware's senator, Joseph R. Biden Jr. Born in Scranton, Pennsylvania, in 1942, he was raised in Wilmington and attended the University of Delaware. After becoming a lawyer, he practiced criminal law in Wilmington, but his ambition was to be the state's

Senator Joseph Biden

senator. In 1972, Biden challenged one-time governor and two-term senator Republican Caleb Boggs. At the age of thirty, Joe Biden became the youngest senator elected by the people in U.S. history.

Preserving History for the Future

Delaware people have long treasured the signs of their fascinating past throughout the state. More than many people in other states, they have worked to preserve that past. The estates and gifts of several industrialists, in addition to the du Pont family, are being put to public use in museums, education centers, meeting halls, parks, and libraries.

The population of Delaware has been growing throughout the state, though certainly not evenly. Most people live within an easy distance of Wilmington, so the care and preservation of that city will remain high on the public agenda of the state. The southern part of the state is more traditional, moving more slowly to make changes.

President Bill Clinton recently reminded Delawareans that Thomas Jefferson had given the state the nickname of the Diamond State. He added that Jefferson, "being as he was a modern thinker," might have said to his Delaware audience: "Delaware is

like a silicon chip—small, but having within it enormous inherent value; namely, the power to shape the future. You have always looked to the future, from the time you became the first state to ratify the Constitution."

Hagley Mills, once a DuPont gunpowder company, is now preserved as a museum.

CHAPTER FIVE

A Great Bit of Coast

Delaware is the second-smallest state in the nation in area, with a total area of 2,397 square miles (6,208 square kilometers). It is 96 miles (154.5 km) long and varies in width from only 9 miles (15 km) near Odessa to 39 miles (63 km) in the south.

This little state lies on the northeastern portion of the Delmarva Peninsula between Chesapeake Bay and Delaware Bay. The name is an abbreviation of the three states that occupy the peninsula—Delaware, Maryland, and Virginia.

Delaware has only 28 miles (45 km) of coastline, the distance from its southern border with Maryland to Cape Henlopen along the

The Delaware Water Gap

Opposite: Cape Henlopen State Park

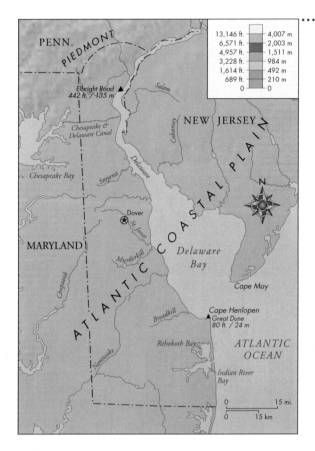

Delaware's topography

Atlantic Ocean. But it has 381 miles (613 km) of shoreline bordering Delaware Bay.

Peculiar Boundaries

Delaware is bordered along straight lines in the west and south by Maryland. On the east, its boundary with New Jersey in Delaware Bay is the navigation channel—the deepest part, through which ships can travel. However, north of Odessa, the border swings eastward to the New Jersey shore, so that the entire river belongs to Delaware. This is the result of a 1935 U.S. Supreme Court decision.

The last boundary—with Pennsylvania in the north—is one of the most unusual boundaries in the United States. It is a partial circle. In 1681, King Charles II of England gave William Penn land north of a 12-mile (19-km) circle with the courthouse at New Castle as the center. In 1701, two surveyors marked the boundary from the Delaware River westward for 120 degrees or two-thirds of a semicircle.

Highs and Lows

The entire Delmarva Peninsula is part of the Atlantic Coastal Plain. The East Coast of North America has a flat area along the seacoast (sometimes called the Tidewater) that stretches westward to the fall line. The fall line is the edge of a region of hard rock over which rivers drop in waterfalls. It is as far as ships can navigate up

Delaware's Geographical Features

Total area; rank	2,397 sq. mi. (6,208 sq km); 49th
Land; rank	1,955 sq. mi. (5,063 sq km); 49th
Water; rank	442 sq. mi. (1,145 sq km); 41st
Inland water; rank	71 sq. mi. (184 sq km); 49th
Coastal water; rank	371 sq. mi. (960 sq km); 15th
Geographic center	Kent, 11 miles (18 km) south of Dover
Highest point	Ebright Road in New Castle County, 442 feet (135 m)
Lowest point	Sea level along the coast
Largest city	Wilmington
Population; rank	668,696 (1990 census); 46th
Record high temperature	110°F (43°C) at Millsboro on July 21, 1930
Record low temperature	–17°F (–27°C) at Millsboro on January 17, 1893
Average July temperature	76°F (24°C)
Average January temperature	35°F (2°C)
Average annual precipitation	45 inches (114 cm)

a river. New York, Philadelphia, Trenton, Wilmington, Baltimore, and Richmond are among the cities located at the fall line. West of the fall line is the Piedmont, the gradually rising ground leading to the Appalachian Mountains.

All but a small northern part of Delaware is in the Coastal Plain. The state lies closer to sea level than any state except Florida. Its average elevation is only 60 feet (18 m). Toward the south, the sand carried by the Delaware River through the bay creates large sand dunes that seem very high compared to the flat marshy land around them. Cape Henlopen State Park near Lewes has a sand dune 80 feet (24 m) high. This Great Dune is the highest sand dune beween Cape Cod in Massachusetts and Cape Hatteras in North Carolina.

Most states have a specific hill or peak that can be identified as being the highest point in the state. In very flat Delaware, the

Along the sand dunes at Cape Henlopen State Park

highest point has been identified as a place on Ebright Road in New Castle County, where the elevation reaches 442 feet (135 m). The lowest point is anywhere along the shore at sea level.

Delaware River and Bay

The Delaware River begins where several small streams gather in the Catskill Mountains of New York and the Pocono Mountains of Pennsylvania. The river's two branches join at Hancock, New York, and then flow through mountains to the Delaware Water Gap, a deep gorge in the Kittatinny Mountains between Pennsylvania and New Jersey. It then enters the Piedmont region heading toward the Coastal Plain.

For much of its length, the river serves as the boundary between Pennsylvania and New York or between Pennsylvania and New Jersey. At Trenton, New Jersey, the widening river becomes tidal and enters Delaware Bay. The river has traveled about 280 miles (451 km) before it enters the bay.

Delaware Bay is the estuary of the Delaware River. An estuary is the mouth of a river where saltwater flows in with the ocean tides and mixes with freshwater coming from the river. The living things in an estuary are usually quite different from the life in the river itself or in the adjoining ocean.

Sunlight reflecting on Delaware Bay

The bay was originally the valley that formed during the ice ages around the lower Delaware River. At that time—up to about 12,000 years ago—so much water was tied up in glaciers that the ocean was much lower. As the glaciers melted, the river valley was "drowned" and the estuary formed.

The bay is partially enclosed by Cape May, the southernmost point of New Jersey, and Cape Henlopen, the easternmost point of Delaware. Cape Henlopen became one of North America's first pieces of public land when William Penn declared it public in 1682.

The Breakwater

The rocks of the Cape Henlopen area were used between 1828 and 1835 to build a breakwater. The 1-mile (1.6-km)-long break-water provides a barrier that shelters boats and protects the town of Lewes from battering by the sea. It also includes a light-house. Young whales can occasionally be seen off the break-water in winter. ■

The Strange Horseshoe Crab

One of the most unusual animals on Earth breeds in the bay off Delaware. Called the horseshoe crab, it isn't really a crab, but an ancient relative of the scorpion. For possibly 300 million to 400 million years—long before dinosaurs ruled Earth—horseshoe crabs have lived in the seas. There are only four species left, and Delaware's is one of them.

Female horseshoe crabs come ashore in spring. Each one lays 80,000 eggs, and the eggs attract numerous shorebirds as they migrate northward (above). The nutritious eggs provide energy for the next part of their long flight to the Arctic.

For thousands of years, the hungry birds did not kill off the ancient crab, but modern life might. The number of breeding adults has plummeted in recent years. There appear to be two reasons. First, the habitat they need for breeding has been shrinking because of the increased development of beach-front property. And, second, the commercial fishing industry has discovered that horseshoe crabs make wonderful bait for eels and conchs. University of Delaware biologists hope to develop synthetic crab bait for the sea creatures, thus preserving the real horseshoe crabs. ■

Delaware Bay has bad shoals on its eastern side. Shoals are accumulations of sand or other sediment on the ocean bottom as it rises toward shore. These sandbars can prevent boats from reaching shore and can even be dangerous. This is why the settlement of New Jersey came from the ocean, rather than from the bay. It also meant that when ships entered the bay, they tended to head toward the western shore—Delaware.

Wetlands—both saltwater and freshwater—cover a considerable portion of the state. The largest, called Great Cypress Swamp, lies on the southern border and is shared by Maryland. This swamp features the distinctly southern bald cypress trees known for their gnarled "knees," which grow like aerial roots out of the water. Nearby Trap Pond State Park includes the northernmost natural stand of bald cypress.

The Atlantic Flyway

Just as important as the waters of Delaware Bay are the tidal marshes along its shores. The marshes provide spawning areas for fish and excellent hiding places for the young before they venture out into the bay. They also provide feeding grounds for birds.

For hundreds of thousands of years, birds have followed certain routes on their annual migrations. These regular routes, called flyways, developed because food sources were reliable along the path. In recent decades, naturalists have shown that if too much development occurs along a flyway, the number of birds shrinks.

The marshes along both sides of Delaware Bay are important resources for birds flying the Atlantic flyway. More than 50 miles (80 km) of shoreline and 126,000 acres (51,012 hectares) of

Snow Geese

One of the natural treasures of Delaware is the great concentration of snow geese that live at Bombay Hook National Wildlife Refuge each winter. Snow geese are large white geese with black wingtips, pink legs, and a pink bill. They breed in Greenland and spend the winter around Delaware and Chesapeake Bays. More geese live around Bombay Hook than anywhere else in North America—usually more than 100,000 birds. ■

Delaware Bay marshland is regarded as wetland of international importance because of its importance to wildlife.

Bombay Hook National Wildlife Refuge is an important link in the Atlantic flyway. Made up of marshland, the area was used by Dutch settlers for trapping muskrats and hunting waterfowl. The name Bombay Hook evolved from the Dutch name *Boompies Hoock,* or little-tree point. It has been a national refuge since 1937, when it became clear that the number of waterfowl taking the Atlantic flyway was declining.

Great egrets in the Bombay Hook National Wildlife Refuge

Delaware's parks and forests

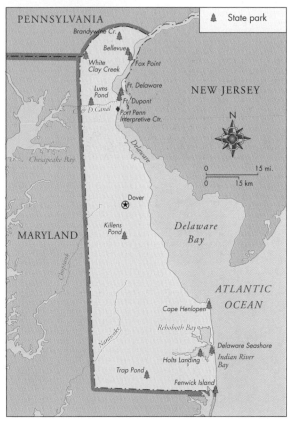

Near Milton, south of Bombay Hook, is Prime Hook National Wildlife Refuge, also consisting of wetlands. Prime Hook's water level can be controlled so that plenty of feed is available when needed by migrating birds. It is also home to many turtles and other reptiles and amphibians.

The drier portions of both refuges are home to such mammals as gray and red foxes, deer, muskrats, and woodchucks. Lucky hikers can sometimes see river otters playing in the open streams of the wetlands.

Other Rivers

Brandywine Creek, which is shared with Pennsylvania, was a source of water power for early colonists. The river was named for

**Fall foliage along
Brandywine Creek**

Andren Brantwyn, a Swedish colonist. Starting about 1740, Quakers used the flowing water to turn wheat-grinding stones and made the colony the breadbasket of the region. Around the Brandywine are the small hills that make up Delaware's only heights. (Many waterways called creeks in Delaware would certainly be called rivers elsewhere.)

The Brandywine flows into the river the Dutch called the Minquas and the Swedes called the Christina, after their queen. This river was deep enough to take a large ship inland for several miles to the fall line. When the ship could go no farther, the Swedes settled Christinaham. Wilmington was founded in the same location in 1731.

The Mispillion River divides Kent and Sussex Counties. It also divides the small city of Milford, which got its name from the mills built on the river. For a while the river, too, was called the Milford.

While most of the state's rivers drain into the Delaware River or into Delaware Bay, the Nanticoke and the Choptank in the south run southwest into Chesapeake Bay. There they widen into important arms of the bay. Chesapeake Bay is also at one end of the vitally important Chesapeake and Delaware Canal. This canal is often regarded as the boundary between Delaware's industrial north and rural south.

The Flowing Kills

Several of Delaware's rivers have "kill" in their names. This was an old Dutch word for "river." Murderkill in the south was originally called Mother River by the Dutch, but their word for mother was "murther," which looked to the English like "murder." ∎

A lazy day on the Nanticoke River

**Ballooning above Indian
River Bay**

Bays and Beaches

From Cape Henlopen south to the Maryland border, the Atlantic shore is lined with sandy beaches. In three places along this 25-mile (40-km) stretch, bays make deep indentations in the coast.

Rehoboth Bay and Indian River Bay form fingerlike recreation areas, with plenty of waterfront for vacation homes, though the bays are very shallow. A small canal opened in 1913 connects Rehoboth Bay and Lewes. Another canal connects Indian River Bay and Assawoman Bay (the name is a form of the Indian name *Assawomet*) in the south.

**Delaware Seashore
State Park**

The narrow barrier beach that protects Rehoboth Bay from the fury of the Atlantic is Delaware Seashore State Park. A similarly narrow strip farther south is 3-mile (5-km)-long Fenwick Island State Park. It protects Assawoman Bay, which Delaware shares with Maryland. A lighthouse stands on Fenwick Island.

Parklands

As early as 1682, William Penn declared the area that is now Cape Henlopen State Park public land. In addition, the state has twelve other state parks. One wonderful advantage of Delaware's small size is that nowhere in the state is more than a two-hour drive from a state park.

For decades, the Pennsylvania Railroad filled in land along the Delaware River, and it gradually became seriously polluted. In 1958, many Delawareans succeeded in getting the railroad to turn the long, narrow strip of land over to the public. The hazardous materials in the soil have been capped and the land has been recycled into open parkland as Fox Point State Park.

This park is the northern end of the 90-mile (145-km)-long Coastal Heritage Greenway, which stretches down to Cape Henlopen. A greenway is a long and usually narrow sec-

The Coastal Heritage Greenway provides a beautiful route for bicycling.

tion of open land that both wildlife and people can use without venturing into populated areas.

Delaware is the only state without a single National Park Service site. It has no national parks, no national monuments, and not even a national historical monument.

Pollution Threats

It has been estimated that 15,000 species of plants and animals depend on Delaware Bay and the surrounding rivers and marshes. All these living things are threatened when their habitat is threatened.

The biggest threat to Delaware Bay, the river, and the marshes is pollution. By the beginning of the 1700s, the water was already being polluted, and it carried many water-borne diseases. As industrial towns grew along the river in the nineteenth and twentieth centuries, much of the waste from the factories was dumped into the river system.

By 1950, large parts of the river, especially around Philadelphia, were declared "dead." Nothing could live in such badly polluted water. Delaware, Pennsylvania, New York, New Jersey, and the federal government joined in an effort to clean up the river and the bay.

It's working. Twice as many species of fish live in the waterway as in 1969. However, the water is not yet safe for swimming because of chemicals in the sediment and high bacteria levels.

The biggest continuing danger other than development is petroleum. Delaware Bay is the largest oil-transfer port of entry on the East Coast. Billions of barrels of oil are moved through the bay annually.

Delmarva Climate

As a mid-Atlantic state, Delaware has a moderate climate. During the summer, its average temperature is 76 degrees Fahrenheit (24° Celsius), with the coastal temperature about 10°F cooler than the temperature inland. In winter, the average temperature is about freezing—32°F (0°C). The temperature along the coast is about 10°F warmer. The state receives about 45 inches (114 cm) of precipitation each year.

The peninsula is also a transition zone between northern and southern plant life. Around Wilmington, the trees and other plants resemble those of Pennsylvania and New York. In the southern part of the state, the plants are more like those of Maryland and Virginia.

Delaware's moderate climate offers many warm, sunny days.

CHAPTER SIX

The Little State with a Big Story

Eleutherian Mills

Delaware has no large cities. Wyoming, West Virginia, Vermont, North Dakota, and Maine are the only other states that have no larger cities. Delaware's largest city is Wilmington, with about 71,000 people. But its history and its wonderful museums are enough to satisfy any fan of cities.

The du Pont Estates

The du Pont family members of the nineteenth century, like many other industrial giants, believed in using their vast wealth to create beautiful settings for themselves and their friends. The twentieth-century du Ponts carried on that tradition, but they began turning their estates into places for the public. In some cases, they set up foundations that run and restore the houses

Opposite: The Hagley Museum

and gardens. In other cases, the state itself came to own the properties.

Hagley Museum and Library on Brandywine Creek is the site of the original DuPont gunpowder works. Not just a museum, Hagley is a community resource. It is open for a summer concert series—classical, rock, and country—and hundreds of children have enjoyed summer day camp there. The first home on the grounds of the gunpowder works was Eleutherian Mills, built in 1803 by E. I. du Pont. The family lived in it until the 1950s, when they began creating the museum.

Nemours (named after the family's original French chateau) is the beautiful 300-acre (121-ha) estate of Alfred I. du Pont. Built about 1910, the pink stone house has 102 rooms. It looks in every way like the estate that Pierre Samuel du Pont would have left behind in France. Much of its structure and its decor came from the finest palaces and estates in Europe.

Alfred I. du Pont wrote in his will, "It has been my firm conviction throughout life that it is the duty of everyone in the world to do what is within his power to alleviate human suffering." When he died in 1935, he left much of his wealth to the Nemours Foundation, which created a hospital for crippled children on the grounds of the estate. In recent years, the foundation has established children's health clinics across the United States.

Bellevue State Park covers 328 acres (133 ha) along the Delaware River. It surrounds the beautiful Bellevue Hall mansion developed by William H. du Pont Jr. and acquired by the state in 1976. The hall is a replica of President James Madison's home—Montpelier—and the grounds are great for picnicking.

Some of the beautiful du Pont houses are not open to the public. For example, Granogue, the chateau of Irnèe du Pont, can be seen only from the road.

Granogue after a snowfall

Winterthur

Winterthur, just outside of Wilmington, is one of the most exciting museums in America. Named for a town in Switzerland, it was originally an elaborate farmhouse bought by Senator Henry A. du Pont and his son, Henry Francis du Pont. Henry Francis began gathering what became the world's biggest collection of American furniture and decorative items made between 1640 and 1860.

In 1951, Henry Francis moved into a smaller villa and turned the mansion into the Henry Francis du Pont Winterthur Museum. The building is nine stories high and has 180 rooms decorated as

Winterthur Gardens

they might have been during various periods and places. At Christmas, every room takes on a special flavor. There is even a "Touch It" room in which children can go. The gardens surrounding the museum cover 985 acres (399 ha) and are planted with many special displays, although the basic effect is of a garden created by nature.

Elsewhere in Wilmington

Wilmington was founded in 1731 by Thomas Willing, an Englishman who married a Swedish woman. He laid out some streets and called his town after himself—Willingtown. The name was changed to Wilmington in 1739 when King George II granted it a royal charter. It is named after the earl of Wilmington, an English politician who was briefly an official for the king. The town did not really develop, though, until Quakers arrived in the area and their flour mills began to flourish. For some years, the ports of the Wilmington area were the landing sites of slave ships, but the Quaker influence led to the outlawing of slave auctions before the Revolutionary War.

In 1802, the du Ponts began their businesses on the Brandywine as did the Bancrofts and the Gilpins, who made textiles and paper. William Poole Bancroft was a major benefactor of the growing city, supporting a park system—much of it on land he donated—and a public library.

The area now called Willingtown Square contains five historic buildings that were moved from elsewhere in the city in 1976. They date from between 1748 and 1801, the period during which milling and shipping were the main economic activities of the Wilmington area. The buildings are still in use as offices and meetingrooms.

Built in 1798, Old Town Hall was Wilmington's jail and the city's offices, but it also served as the center of political and social activities until the Civil War. Underneath the welcoming halls, however, were jail cells where prisoners lived on bread and water.

The Delaware Art Museum was founded around the collection of original illustra-

Inside the Delaware Art Museum

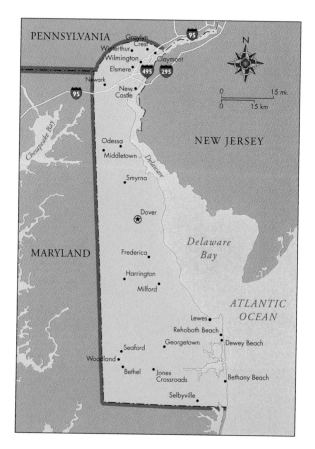

Delaware's cities and interstates

tions by Howard Pyle. It also contains work of other illustrators such as N. C. Wyeth, Frank Schoonover, and Maxfield Parrish. The museum has one of the finest collections of the romantic paintings of the mid-1800s known as Pre-Raphaelite art.

Old Brandywine Village in Wilmington lies along Brandywine Creek. The original flour mills were built there, using the waters of the creek to turn the grindstones. These mills helped turn Delaware into one of the main "Flour Colonies." The mill owners' stone houses stand nearby. Also along the creek is a park designed by Frederick Law Olmsted, who designed New York City's Central Park and the Columbian Exposition on Chicago's lakefront. Brandywine Zoo is located near this park.

The Christina River flowing through Wilmington made the city an important port and an industrial center. After World War II, the waterfront was allowed to deteriorate but recently the city has restored its waterfront buildings to emphasize art and history. A beautiful walk 1.5 miles (2 km) long is being completed. As part of the on-going $70-million revitalization of downtown Wilmington, the First USA Riverfront Arts Center opened in 1998. Formerly an abandoned navy yard, it has a new exhibit and convention center.

A replica of the *Kalmar Nyckel* in the Port of Wilmington

New Castle—The First Capital

Only a few miles south but 200 years back in time is New Castle, the state's first capital. The fledgling town was Fort Casimir. Peter Stuyvesant laid out its central park. Once a year, the residents invite the public into private homes that are closed to visitors the rest of the year. A Day in Old New Castle happens on the third Saturday in May.

Between 1651 and 1681, New Castle was owned by five countries (some of them twice) and its name was changed four times. Then in 1777, the state capital was moved to Dover and in 1881, the county seat was moved to Wilmington. New Castle was left to the attentions of those who loved living there or couldn't afford to move elsewhere.

The Old Dutch House in New Castle

The Old Dutch House, built in the late 1600s when New Castle was under English control, stands out as an example of the home of a middle-class Dutch family. New Castle Court House, built in 1732, is regarded as the birthplace of Delaware State. It housed both the colonial and the first state assemblies.

Historic New Castle stands apart from the rest of the city, which is an active town. It has cars, modern businesses, and schools. More than 100,000 people a day cross the Delaware Memorial Bridge between Interstate 295 and the New Jersey Turnpike—the longest twin-span suspension bridge in the world.

Pea Patch Island lies in the Delaware River south of New Castle. It is occupied by Fort Delaware and is reached by a ferry. This state park has a huge population of wading birds, especially herons and egrets.

West of New Castle is Newark, where the University of Delaware is located. The town's name is pronounced New-ARK, which is the way the name was once spelled, instead of NEW-urk, as in New Jersey. Located near the junction of Pennsylvania, Maryland, and Delaware, it is only slightly smaller than Dover.

South of the Canal

Although the southern edge of New Castle County is still farther south, the Chesapeake and Delaware Canal separates north and south Delaware. The northern section is all business, industry, and busy highways. The southern section is still rural and fairly peaceful, although tourism is rapidly expanding along the beaches.

Odessa in central New Castle County south of the canal is located on Appoquinimink Creek. Originally called Cantwell's

Odessa's Wilson-Warner House

Bridge, it was a grain-shipping port in the nineteenth century. In 1855, the town changed its name to Odessa, hoping that it would become as famous as the grain-shipping seaport of Odessa in the Ukraine. The town has many well-preserved old houses. Three of them, along with a hotel, are known as the historic houses of Odessa. They are owned and exhibited by Winterthur.

The Capital

With fewer than 30,000 residents, Dover is one of the smallest state capitals in the United States. It is located on the St. Jones River (no one knows where the name came from), in Kent, the middle county. William Penn made the original plan for Dover, calling for it to be built around Meeting House Square. The green is still a central part of Dover. The Delaware Arch- aeology Museum now occupies a Presbyterian church built near the square in 1790.

Penn did not expect Dover to become the capital of the state, but it did so in 1777 because the colonials feared that their capital at New Castle would be attacked by the British navy from the Delaware River. The Old State House was the capitol until 1933. At that time, the Legislative Hall was built, and official offices of the state were moved there. The government buildings, especially around Capital Square, have large, green lawns that adjoin the town green. The city is also home to Dover Air Force Base.

A peaceful front porch in Dover

His Master's Voice

Eldridge Reeves Johnson grew up in Dover but, as an adult, he moved across the bay to Camden, New Jersey. There, in 1901, he founded the Victor Talking Machine Company, which made the early phonographs called Victrolas that took the United States by storm. The company later became RCA Victor, with a symbol of a little black-and-white terrier listening to "His Master's Voice" coming out of the horn of a Victrola (right). The Johnson Victrola Museum in Dover features some of the early "talking machines" that Johnson invented, as well as 15,000 recordings. ■

Barratt's Chapel, where the American Methodist Church was formed

At Jones Neck on the St. Jones River stands the home of John Dickinson, "Penman of the American Revolution" and a president (governor) of the state. Although Dickinson freed all his slaves, the estate still has an old slave house near the brick mansion.

Near Frederica, south of Dover Air Force Base is Barratt's Chapel, where Francis Asbury and Dr. Thomas Coke, representing John Wesley, met in 1784. Here, they organized the American Methodist Church.

Harrington, farther south, is the site of the Delaware State Fair held annually in July since 1919. The fair reminds those who may forget that Delaware is still very much an agricultural state.

Sussex County

Georgetown is the county seat of Sussex County. One of the unusual events in Georgetown is called Return Day. In the old days, when commmunications were slow, people gathered in Georgetown to learn the results of an election. Today, the celebration still goes on after each election day.

Lewes is an historic city that has modernized itself to attract vacationers to the beaches and nature trails of nearby Cape Henlopen State Park. Lewes is the best place to experience Delaware's early Dutch history, especially historic Zwaanendael House. Tours

The Cape May–Lewes
Ferry crossing the
Delaware Bay

of Delaware Bay lighthouses leave by boat from Lewes. Some lighthouses are said to be haunted.

Lewes is the farthest north of Delaware's ocean beaches. However, other great beaches are reached by the Cape May–Lewes Ferry, which leaves from Lewes about every two hours and more often in summer. The ferry crosses the mouth of Delaware Bay to the southernmost tip of New Jersey.

The entire village of Bethel near the Nanticoke River in the southwestern corner of the state is on the national register of historic places. It was formerly a shipyard for schooners that sailed up and down the coast.

The Beaches

You might think that Rehoboth Beach, with its history attached to religion, was given its religious name by the Methodists. However, the name was really taken from the bay, which was named Rehoboth Bay back in the 1700s by a Virginia sea captain who

A Ferry Instead of a Bridge

A car ferry that is actually part of the state highway system crosses the Nanticoke River between Woodland and Bethel. It has been in use since probably before 1671 and may be the oldest continuously used ferry in the United States. Until 1931, it was poled across the river by hand. Since then, it has been under the control of the Delaware Department of Transportation and a motorized ferry crosses the 500 feet (153 m) of river in three minutes. ■

placed it on a map back. Its Hebrew name is most often translated as "room enough."

It's a good thing that there's "room enough" because the Rehoboth Beach area has been called the nation's summer capital, due to the number of people who go there from Washington, D.C., on holiday. Many of them have built summer homes in the town, giving it some very fancy areas. The square-mile resort has only a few thousand year-round residents, but an estimated 6 million visitors come to the little community each year.

Rehoboth has one of the last beach boardwalks on the Atlantic. This raised wooden sidewalk was built in 1884 to keep the ladies' shoes from filling with sand. Damaged by a storm in 1991, it was restored the following year. Along the boardwalk are motels, amusements, and snack-food and other restaurants.

South of Rehoboth Beach is Dewey Beach. This beach attracts a little different crowd than Rehoboth Beach because in addition to being on the

Sailboats along the beach at Fenwick Island

ocean, it also fronts on Rehoboth Bay. The bay provides protected water for watercraft.

Starting at Bethany Beach and going all the way to Ocean City, Maryland, the long seafront beach is lined with condominiums and hotels. Fenwick Island, where a lighthouse is still in operation, is the last Delaware beach.

CHAPTER SEVEN

Government Old and New

Legislative Hall

Just two months after the Declaration of Independence was signed, Delawareans held a convention to redesign their own government. Each county elected representatives to the convention. The document describing the state's new government was the first state constitution written by people elected to write such a document.

That first constitution called for a president who was under the control of the Privy Council. The members were chosen by the General Assembly. The assembly could do as it pleased; the laws it passed needed no one's approval. However, the assembly was split into an upper and a lower house, and each house could prevent the other from taking action. Only men who owned land could vote.

After the new United States Constitution was signed in 1787, Delaware set about rewriting its own constitution, which went into effect in 1792. The name was officially changed to the State of Delaware, and the two houses of the assembly were named the

Opposite: Woodburn, the governor's mansion

senate and the house of representatives. Most important, though, was the change back to a governor elected directly by the people and with real authority to make decisions. In this constitution every white male taxpayer could vote; he didn't have to own land. In addition, a person no longer had to be a Protestant to be elected to the assembly.

Several attempts were made to rewrite the constitution in the 1800s as Wilmington became increasingly important and needed better representation in the General Assembly. Finally, in 1897, a new and very detailed constitution was adopted. It has been used, with many amendments—especially about proportional representation in the General Assembly—since then. In that constitution, the governor was finally given the right to veto—or turn down—bills passed by the legislature. The men who wrote the new constitution talked about giving the vote to women, but rejected the idea. Delaware is the only state that can have its constitution amended without approval by the citizens.

Branches of Government

At the head of Delaware's government is the governor, who is elected for one four-year term, although he or she can be reelected for one more term. Despite the fact that Delaware once tried to make the "president" a powerless figure, Delaware's governor resembles governors in most states today. The 1897 constitution created the position of lieutenant governor, who can take over the governor's position if necessary. The lieutenant governor also serves as president of the senate. He or she can be reelected more than once.

Delaware's Governors

Name	Party	Term	Name	Party	Term
John McKinly	None	1777	William Tharp	Dem.	1847–1851
Thomas McKean	None	1777	William H. Ross	Dem.	1851–1855
George Read	None	1777–1778	Peter F. Causey	Am.	1855–1859
Caesar Rodney	None	1778–1781	William Burton	Dem.	1859–1863
John Dickinson	None	1781–1782	William Cannon	Union	1863–1865
John Cook	None	1782–1783	Gove Saulsbury	Dem.	1865–1871
Nicholas Van Dyke	None	1783–1786	James Ponder	Dem.	1871–1875
Thomas Collins	None	1786–1789	John P. Cochran	Dem.	1875–1879
Jehu Davis	None	1789	John W. Hall	Dem.	1879–1883
Joshua Clayton	Fed.	1789–1796	Charles C. Stockley	Dem.	1883–1887
Gunning Bedford Sr.	Fed.	1796–1797	Benjamin T. Biggs	Dem.	1887–1891
Daniel Rogers	Fed.	1797–1799	Robert J. Reynolds	Dem.	1891–1895
Richard Bassett	Fed.	1799–1801	Joshua H. Marvil	Rep.	1895
James Sykes	Fed.	1801–1802	William T. Watson	Dem.	1895–1897
David Hall	Dem.-Rep.	1802–1805	Ebe W. Tunnell	Dem.	1897–1901
Nathaniel Mitchell	Fed.	1805–1808	John Hunn	Rep.	1901–1905
George Truitt	Fed.	1808–1811	Preston Lea	Rep.	1905–1909
Joseph Haslet	Dem.-Rep.	1811–1814	Simeon S. Pennewill	Rep.	1909–1913
Daniel Rodney	Fed.	1814–1817	Charles R. Miller	Rep.	1913–1917
John Clark	Fed.	1817–1820	John G. Townsend Jr.	Rep.	1917–1921
Jacob Stout	Fed.	1820–1821	William D. Denney	Rep.	1921–1925
John Collins	Dem.-Rep.	1821–1822	Robert P. Robinson	Rep.	1925–1929
Caleb Rodney	Fed.	1822–1823	C. Douglass Buck	Rep.	1929–1937
Joseph Haslet	Dem.-Rep.	1823	Richard C. McMullen	Dem.	1937–1941
Charles Thomas	Dem.-Rep.	1823–1824	Walter W. Bacon	Rep.	1941–1949
Samuel Paynter	Fed.	1824–1827	Elbert N. Carvel	Dem.	1949–1953
Charles Polk	Fed.	1827–1830	J. Caleb Boggs	Rep.	1953–1960
David Hazzard	Am. Rep.	1830–1833	David P. Buckson	Rep.	1960–1961
Caleb P. Bennett	Dem.	1833–1836	Elbert N. Carvel	Dem.	1961–1965
Charles Polk	Whig	1836–1837	Charles L. Terry Jr.	Dem.	1965–1969
Cornelius P. Comegys	Whig	1837–1841	Russell W. Peterson	Rep.	1969–1973
William B. Cooper	Whig	1841–1845	Sherman W. Tribbitt	Dem.	1973–1977
Thomas Stockton	Whig	1845–1846	Pierre S. du Pont IV	Rep.	1977–1985
Joseph Maull	Whig	1846	Michael N. Castle	Rep.	1985–1993
William Temple	Whig	1846–1847	Thomas Carper	Dem.	1993–

The senate chambers of the Old State House

Ghosts and Slaves

The official home of Delaware's governor is Woodburn, a beautiful Georgian house built in 1790, although the state did not acquire it until 1966. Tradition holds that there was once a tunnel going from a secret room in the basement out to the St. Jones River, where runaway slaves waited for river transport into Pennsylvania and freedom. Oddly, though, the ghost for which Woodburn is known is not that of a slave but of an older gentlemen in powdered wig and knee breeches. A guest in the house first saw him in 1815. ■

Delaware's legislature is the General Assembly. It is made up of a house of representatives, with forty-one members elected for two-year terms, and a senate, with twenty-one members elected for four-year terms. Half of the senate seats are open in each general election.

The first woman to serve in the state legislature was Florence M. Hanby, elected in 1924. The first African-American elected to the General Assembly was William J. Winchester in 1948—a Republican from Wilmington.

The judicial branch of government is headed by the state supreme court. It has a chief justice and four associate justices with all members appointed by the governor, and confirmed by the senate, for a term of twelve years. Within the judicial branch are several separate courts. A superior court, a family court, a court of common pleas (civil cases not involving the state), and

Delaware's State Government

Executive Branch

```
                        Governor
    ┌──────────┬──────────┼──────────┬──────────────┐
Lieutenant   State     Attorney   Auditor of    Insurance
Governor    Treasurer   General    Accounts    Commissioner
```

Legislative Branch

| Senate | House of Representatives |

Judicial Branch

```
          Supreme Court
          Superior Court
         Court of Chancery
           Family Court
        Court of Common Pleas
```

justice of the peace courts make up Delaware's court system. In addition, there is the Court of Chancery, which is an old type of court from England. This court hears cases involving corporations as well as civil rights cases. The governor also appoints the judges in the other Delaware courts.

The Old State House
was built in 1792.

The Old State House in Dover was originally built in 1792 as the state capitol. Although the state house is used for ceremonial occasions, the real work of the state government is carried on in a newer building called Legislative Hall.

Two U.S. senators elected for six-year terms represent Delaware in Congress—though until 1916 they were appointed. It also has one U.S. representative, elected for a two-year term. Though Delaware has only one representative, Congress has learned not to ignore the state because it has an influence far beyond its small size. The state also serves as an indicator of presidential politics—Delawareans have voted for every winning

The Whipping Post

In 1717, the Lower Counties instituted the whipping post as an officially recognized form of punishment. When Delaware became a state, the laws kept the whipping post for most crimes, especially theft. In addition to being publicly whipped with a cat-o'-nine-tails, the convicted criminal had to stand in a pillory, with head and arms held immobile in a framework. The pillory was outlawed in 1905, but whipping was mandatory until 1925 (except for women, who had been excused in 1889). After 1925, it was up to the judge to decide whether the whipping post was used or not. It was last used in 1952, though it was another twenty years before Delaware became the last state in the Union to eliminate official whipping. ■

presidential candidate since 1952. The state has three electoral votes, used in electing the president and vice president.

The Counties

The state is divided into three counties. The largest is Sussex County in the south, with 950 square miles (2,461 sq km). In the center is Kent County with 594 square miles (1,538 sq km). Farthest north is New Castle County with 439 square miles (1,137 sq km). Each county is as wide as the whole state.

William Penn gave Kent and Sussex Counties their names. Sussex had first been called Hoerekill (changed by the English to Whorekill) and then Deal, and Kent had been St. Jones County.

New Castle in the north is part of the Philadelphia industrial urban area. It stretches from the semicircular border with Pennsylvania south to the Smyrna River. Wilmington, Delaware's largest city and New Castle's county seat since 1881, is located there, along with most factories.

The central county is Kent, between the Smyrna and Mispillion Rivers. Dover, which is at its heart, is both the state capital and the county seat. Beyond Dover, the landscape is quite rural.

The southernmost county, south of the Mispillion River, is Sussex County. It is

Delaware's counties

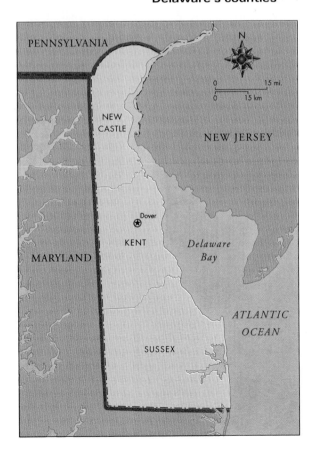

almost all farmland and marsh. Much of its land is dedicated to raising poultry. Georgetown is the county seat.

The counties are not divided into townships as they are in
other states, but into "hundreds"—a term that dates back to Alfred
the Great in England. It is the only state where this term for county
division is still used.

The counties collect property taxes, but most of the state's taxes
are income taxes, both personal and corporate. Because well over
half of all large corporations throughout the nation are incorporated in Delaware, corporate taxes make up a large percentage of the
state's funds. Delaware has a state lottery, from which funds go into
the state's general treasury. They are not allotted to specific purposes.

Like many states, Delaware ignored, for many years, the fact
that the state was growing without any controls on the growth. But

Delaware's State Song
"Our Delaware"

Delaware's state song was adopted in 1925. Each of the first three verses honors one county. These verses were written by George B. Hynson. Donn Devine wrote an additional verse in praise of the state and its citizens' loyalty. Will M. S. Brown set the poem to music.

Chorus
Oh our Delaware! Our beloved
    Delaware!
For the sun is shining over our
    beloved Delaware,
Oh our Delaware! Our beloved
    Delaware!
Here's the loyal son that
    pledges,
Faith to good old Delaware.

Oh the hills of dear New Castle,
and the smiling vales between,
When the corn is all in tassel,
And the meadowlands are
    green;
Where the cattle crop the
    clover,
And its breath is in the air,
While the sun is shining over
Our beloved Delaware.

(Chorus)

Where the wheat fields break
    and billow,
In the peaceful land of Kent,
Where the toiler seeks his pil-
    low,
With the blessings of content;
Where the bloom that tints the
    peaches,
Cheeks of merry maidens share,
And the woodland chorus
    preaches
A rejoicing Delaware.

(Chorus)

Dear old Sussex visions linger,
Of the holly and the pine,
Of Henlopens jeweled finger,
Flashing out across the brine;

Of the gardens and the
    hedges,
And the welcome waiting
    there,
For the loyal son that pledges
Faith to good old Delaware.

(Chorus)

From New Castle's rolling
    meadows,
Through the fair rich fields of
    Kent,
To the Sussex shores hear
    echoes,
Of the pledge we now present;
Liberty and Independence,
We will guard with loyal care,
And hold fast to freedom's
    presence,
In our home state Delaware.

Delaware is so small that whatever development is done in one part affects the whole state. In 1995, Governor Thomas Carper brought back a statewide planning process called Shaping Delaware's Future.

Delaware's State Symbols

State bird: Blue hen chicken The blue hen chicken (above) was adopted as the state bird on April 14, 1939. During the Revolutionary War, a company of men from Kent County carried with them into battle some particularly vicious fighting cocks of a variety called blue hen. Since much of a soldier's time is spent waiting, the officers and men whiled away time by holding cockfights, which were usually won by the blue hen chickens. When it came to fighting, the men from Delaware were said to be as fierce as their blue hen chickens.

State tree: American holly American holly, also called Christmas holly, was adopted as the state tree on May 1, 1939. It is an important forest tree with dark, thorn-edged leaves and red berries.

State flower: Peach blossom Adopted by the state legislature in May 9, 1895, the peach blossom was chosen to honor the 800,000 peach trees in the state.

State fish: Weakfish Weakfish (also called sea trout and yellow-fin trout) was chosen by the legislature (despite its name) in recognition of the importance of sport fishing to Delaware. Adopted in 1981.

State beverage: Milk Milk was chosen in recognition of the importance of agriculture to the state's history.

State mineral: Sillimanite Sillimanite, adopted on March 24, 1977, is a pale green or brownish aluminum silicate glasslike mineral that forms needlelike crystals. It is found primarily in Delaware. It was named for Benjamin Silliman of Yale University, though it is also called fibrolite.

State insect: Ladybug This insect (left) was lobbied for by elementary schoolchildren and adopted by the legislature on April 25, 1974.

Delaware's State Flag and Seal

DECEMBER 7, 1787

The design of the state flag was adopted on July 24, 1913. Its main colors are colonial blue and buff, which is described as the colors of George Washington's uniform. These are the state colors. A diamond of buff on a colonial blue background bears the coat of arms of the state. Below the diamond are the words "December 7, 1787," when Delaware became the first state to ratify the U.S. Constitution. Below the symbols is the state motto: "Liberty and Independence."

The state seal was first adopted on January 17, 1777, and also displays the coat of arms. The inscription around it says "Great Seal of the State of Delaware" and the dates 1793, 1847, and 1907, years when the seal was modified. Among the symbols used in the coat of arms are several for agriculture (wheat sheaf, corn, farmer, and ox), plus a militiaman, a ship, and water (representing the Delaware River). ■

CHAPTER EIGHT

Chemistry, Corporations, and Chickens

Delaware is the fifth-smallest state in population, but it has the fifth-highest income level in the nation. This happy situation occurs for three main reasons: easy access to major East Coast markets, the chemical companies based on DuPont, and the willingness of state officials to turn Delaware into the Corporate Capital of the World.

Inside a chicken house

Historically, though—and even today in terms of land use—the main occupation of Delaware citizens has been agriculture. The land is so level that only the marshland cannot be plowed and planted.

Because the major East Coast cities are within easy distance of Delaware, the state's products can quickly be distributed. In 1997, Amazon.com, the online bookseller, established its East Coast distribution center in New Castle.

Agricultural Booms

The average farm in Delaware is small, as befits a tiny state—only about 235 acres (95 ha). The largest planted crop is soybeans, followed by corn and various grains.

The original settlers concentrated on growing wheat and corn. In addition, Delaware's transitional climate made it a natural in the

Opposite: A soybean farm

Products from the Bay

Some of the products distributed from Delaware come from Delaware Bay. The bay has long been the source of much of the United States's supply of oysters. However, in recent years, the oyster beds have been overworked and polluted, and supplies are shrinking. Today, the Delaware Bay is more apt to provide clams and crabs as well as shad and menhaden. ■

1800s for growing peach trees. Within just a few decades of discovering that fact, Delaware orchards had 4.5 million trees and it had become the Peach State. Unfortunately, much more quickly, between 1890 and 1900, a disease known as peach yellows killed more than half of those trees. Today, Delaware has fewer than half a million trees.

What Delaware Grows and Manufactures

Agriculture	Manufacturing
Broilers	Chemicals
Corn	Transportation equipment
Soybeans	

Delaware Chicken Divan

Chicken is one of Delaware's main products and tastes wonderful in this simple dish.

Ingredients:

      a small pat of butter
  1 can of cream chicken soup (undiluted)
  $\frac{1}{2}$ cup mayonnaise
  2 tablespoons lemon juice
  2 tablespoons chicken broth
  $\frac{1}{2}$ cup Parmesan cheese
  $1\frac{1}{2}$ pounds of broccoli
  $1\frac{1}{2}$ cups chicken (white meat)

Directions:

Butter the inside bottom and sides of a 1 1/2-quart baking dish. Combine cream of chicken soup, mayonnaise, lemon juice, chicken broth, and Parmesan cheese in a separate bowl.

Wash broccoli and cut into spears. Arrange broccoli on the bottom of the baking dish.

Fill pot with water and simmer chicken until cooked through. Cut into bite-sized pieces, then scatter over broccoli. Spoon sauce over the broccoli and chicken.

Bake uncovered at 350°F for 30 minutes.

Serves 4.

The next agricultural boom—one still growing stronger every year—was started in 1920 by a woman named Cecile Steele of Sussex County. In what, looking back, seems a perfectly logical move, she started raising chickens for sale instead of just for their eggs. Today, broiler chickens are the state's most valuable agricultural product. The soybeans and corn grown on the surrounding farmland, mostly in Sussex County, are used primarily to feed those chickens.

Other parts of the country also began to raise chickens, but Delaware had a head start. Perdue Farms, which is headquartered in nearby Maryland, is the nation's second-largest poultry producer. The company processes approximately 45 million pounds (20 million kilograms) of chicken and turkey per week. The number continues to grow as chicken-breast sandwiches and Buffalo wings grow in popularity. Frozen poultry products are sold all over the world.

DuPont Chemicals

America's sixteenth-largest company is the backbone of Delaware. It is E. I. du Pont de Nemours and Company, the largest chemical company in the world. Usually referred to today as DuPont, it has its headquarters in Wilmington and is the largest employer in Delaware.

Delaware's natural resources

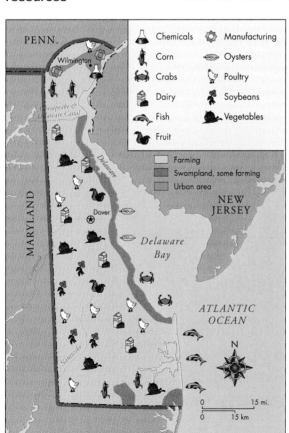

**DuPont headquarters
in Wilmington**

During its first 100 years, DuPont concentrated on producing explosives, the result of having been first in the quality gunpowder business. The explosives weren't just for war, but during the 1800s, the vast forested lands of North America had to be cleared for agriculture and cities. Mining was making fortunes. Roads using gravel and buildings using blocks of stone were being built. Each of those enterprises required explosives in huge quantities. During that first 100 years, the company remained in family hands.

In 1902, Eugene du Pont died without heirs, and the decision was made to sell the company to whomever would pay the most. Alfred Irénée du Pont, a great-grandson of Irénée, bought the company for $12 million. He brought in two cousins, Thomas Coleman du Pont and Pierre Samuel du Pont.

These three great-grandsons also incorporated the firm for the first time. In a corporation, the officers of the company are employees, just like everyone else. This was unusual for du Pont family

Stocking Up

In 1937, a DuPont chemist, Wallace Carothers (left), invented and patented a new plastic that could be made into fibers to replace silk. They called it nylon and envisioned many uses for it, such as stockings, military parachutes, and brush bristles. A new plant was built at Seaford just for the purpose of producing nylon.

When stockings made of the world's first fiber made by chemistry went on the market, American women snapped up 64 million pairs in the first year alone. Silk stockings had always been so expensive that they had to be repaired and kept a long time. Nylon stockings could be thrown away—nice for the women and nice for DuPont. ■

members, but it protected the other people who owned shares in the firm. The firm also began to focus on chemical research. This has been the work of the second 100 years.

The company began to concentrate on research in many fields. Cars had synthetic leather upholstery made by a DuPont company. Home repairs were made with DuPont cement. Motion-picture film was produced by DuPont. Objects, both beautiful and useful, were made with DuPont plastics. More recently, the new brand names of Lucite, Orlon, Lycra, Dacron, Freon, and Mylar have all come from DuPont research. New factories of various kinds were bought or built all over the country. In 1999, DuPont bought Pioneer, the nation's largest seed producer, giving it entry into the important field of genetic engineering for agriculture.

Because of the skilled chemical-manufacturing employees in Delaware, other companies have long been drawn to the area. As the chemical industry of Delaware entered the twenty-first century, Ciba Specialty Chemicals opened a huge plant to make pigments for use in car paints, plastics, and inks in Newport. Zeneca pharmaceuticals of Wilmington, producer of a major cancer-fighting drug, as well as many other products, merged with a similar firm in Sweden called Astra.

In 1917, the du Ponts became very interested in automobiles and started buying stock in General Motors. Eventually, they owned the largest number of shares and Pierre S. du Pont took over management of the firm, turning it into the largest company in the world. In the late 1940s, the federal government began to question whether two of America's greatest companies should be under one ownership. Eventually, in 1962, Pierre du Pont was ordered to sell his stock in General Motors.

Ironically, General Motors is one of two car manufacturers that built assembly plants in Delaware after that (the other is Chrysler). They were taking advantage of Delaware's excellent location for receiving and delivering goods on the East Coast.

Incorporating in Delaware

A business that is incorporated usually has "Inc." after its name. Until 1918, New Jersey was the favorite state of corporations to do their business, but then its laws were tightened. Delaware, which had passed its first general corporation law in 1899, won out by making it easier for companies to incorporate. One of the main benefits is that Delaware's state law does not require that the actual owners of a business be named in public papers. Sometimes people don't want it known that they own part or all of a particular business.

Another attraction for businesses is that Delaware law puts limits on whether the people who own shares in a company can sue the management. In some states, unhappy stockholders can

Motorcycle Museum

An innovative Harley-Davidson dealer in New Castle has opened Mike's Famous Roadside Rest. It's a lot more than a place to sell America's most famous motorcy- cles. It's also a Museum of the Road and a restaurant, all in a large building that looks like Harley-Davidson's 1903 factory in Milwaukee. ■

sue the managers for doing a bad job or for making a decision they don't like.

In addition, the state is so eager to have companies incorporate in Delaware that offices stay open late at night and can even do the paperwork in a few hours if necessary. The Court of Chancery, which deals strictly with businesses, even holds hearings on weekends. Nationally, whenever the news mentions large companies being merged, Delaware's Court of Chancery is almost always involved.

Delaware charges companies incorporated there only moderate taxes, but together they add up to a large portion of the state's bud-

The offices of MBNA America Bank

get. Well over half of the biggest companies in the United States (often called the Fortune 500 because they are named by *Fortune* magazine) are incorporated in Delaware.

In 1980, Delaware raised the limit that can be charged for interest on loans and reduced taxes on banks. That drew banks to the state. MBNA America Bank is the largest independent credit-card distributor in the world. The bank took over many of the downtown buildings in Wilmington and built a new headquarters building. Four large buildings are connected by skywalks. MBNA also bought the historic state courthouse to keep it from being torn down.

CHAPTER NINE

Delaware's People

At the Delmar
Dragway

n mid-1998, Delaware had an estimated population of 743,600,
giving it a rank of forty-sixth among the states. About 65 percent of the people live in New Castle County, around Wilmington.
Northern Delaware is part of the greater Philadelphia metropolitan
area. The south is much like the farms and marshlands of surrounding Maryland and the Delmarva Peninsula.

In the mid-1990s, 80 percent of the people of Delaware were
white, and about 17 percent, were African-American. About one-
third of these lived in the Wilmington area. Most of the remaining
2 percent of Delawareans were Hispanic.

Opposite: Showing a
prize Holstein at the
Delaware State Fair

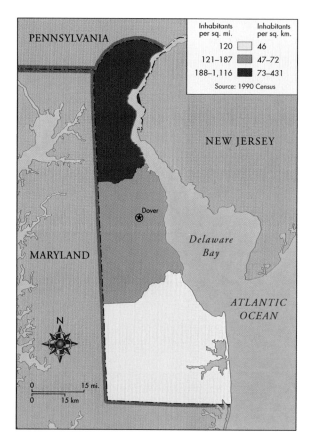

Delaware's population density

Map legend:

Inhabitants per sq. mi.		Inhabitants per sq. km.
120	▢	46
121–187	▨	47–72
188–1,116	▉	73–431

Source: 1990 Census

PENNSYLVANIA

NEW JERSEY

Dover

MARYLAND

Delaware Bay

ATLANTIC OCEAN

N

0   15 mi.
0   15 km

During the 1800s, the main immigrant groups came from Ireland and Germany. One-eighth of all Delaware residents were Irish immigrants. Early in the first part of the twentieth century, more Italians and Poles settled in the state. In recent decades, many Hispanics, especially Puerto Ricans, have come to live in Delaware, primarily in Wilmington.

Education

In its early years, education of Delaware's children was the responsibility of the individual churches. This system didn't reach all children, and in 1829, the legislature approved a public school system. Up until that time, few free blacks had any education, and many white children were expected to work instead of going to school. There was great inequality in the public schools that opened, but at least some were functioning.

The first known school for African-American children was started in Wilmington about 1814. Two years later, a school building for black children was built in that city, but then things seemed to stall. Fifty years later, there were still only seven known schools in the state attended by black children. Not until 1875 did the legislature authorize the spending of tax money on schools for African-Americans—and then, the taxes used came only from African-Americans. The 1897 constitution required by law that

A Wilmington teacher
and her students

black and white children go to separate schools. Nothing was said about providing good schools.

In 1921, state law decreed that there should be adequate schools for blacks, but it confirmed that they had to be separate from schools for white children. Pierre S. du Pont took a leadership role in improving educational facilities in Delaware.

Delaware's schools began to integrate in the 1950s, after the Supreme Court decision. The southern part of the state was slower than the north in integrating its schools. In 1960, a court decision forced the rural areas to speed up the process.

In recent years, Delaware has been at the forefront of the charter school movement. This allows people other than school boards to establish schools, using tax money. In 1999, two schools in Wilmington were named by the federal government to receive funds for major after-school programs. They are part of the Twenty-

Population of Delaware's Major Cities (1990)

Wilmington	71,529
Dover	27,630
Newark	25,098
Brookside	15,307
Claymont	9,800
Wilmington Manor	8,568

First Century Community Learning Centers program to reach unsupervised children throughout the year.

Higher Education

As public schools were getting started, one of the best private schools, Newark Academy, was turned into a college in 1833. The first commencement—graduation ceremony—was held in 1836. However, the college was not properly funded, and it had to close for some years until the legislature agreed to support it, as Delaware College.

In 1914, a women's college was built next door to Delaware College in Newark. Seven years later, the two joined to become the University of Delaware (UD) but it was not fully coeducational until 1944. Today, UD also has a downtown campus in Wilmington, and smaller facilities in Dover, Lewes, and Georgetown. UD has a total of about 21,000 full- and part-time students.

Delaware State University in Dover was founded in 1891 as the Delaware State College for Colored Students. It educated women as well as men from the start, even though the University of

The Star Counter

Annie Jump Cannon (left) was born in Dover in 1863. In the days when women rarely went beyond high school level, she became an astronomer at Harvard University. She worked for many years classifying stars by their spectra—the variable color band made by starlight when it is put through a device called a spectroscope. Her classification of hundreds of thousands of stars formed the basis for much of what we know today about stars. She has been called the Census Taker of the Sky. ■

Delaware's earlier attempt to be coeducational had been dropped. In recent years, Delaware State has had a growing number of white students. Also in Dover is Delaware's oldest private college, Wesley College, which was an outgrowth of the development of Methodism in Delaware. Founded in 1871, it is located in the historic section of Dover.

Widener University originated in Wilmington in 1821 as John Bullock's School for Boys. Today, its main campus is in Chester, Pennsylvania, but it still has a campus in Wilmington that it took

Delaware State University is in Dover.

over from Brandywine Junior College. An important law school, the university college, and a school of hospitality management are located on the Wilmington campus.

The Spiritual Life

Unlike most other colonies, Delaware has never had an established state church. From its earliest days, it has rejoiced in a diversity of religions.

Even though Delaware stopped being a Swedish colony very early, Sweden continued to send Lutheran ministers to Delaware for more than 100 years. Later, under the influence of William Penn, a large number of Quakers settled in Delaware. Because of the Quakers' opposition to war, it was sometimes difficult for the colony to raise the military forces it needed.

Delaware was the site of the founding of the Methodist Church in America. At first, many slaves and former slaves also belonged, but gradually African-Americans felt the need to form their own churches. It was an African-American from Delaware, Richard Allen, who founded the largest black Protestant denomi-

Richard Allen

A Crab Fest

As in other coastal states, one of the great treats of Delaware is steamed crabs. From April to October, they are caught in the ocean and brought in daily. During the other months, they are left to multiply. Crabs are often steamed on the beach in great kettles of boiling water. They are messy to eat, so people dining on crab usually wear bibs and use plenty of napkins while enjoying the succulent white meat. ■

nation, the African Methodist Episcopal Church, in Philadelphia. Today, the Methodist Church is still the largest Protestant Church. The number of Roman Catholics, however, is greater than the number of Methodists.

Among the early German immigrants were some Jews, so a Jewish community has existed in Delaware for well more than 100 years. More recently, many Jews have come from Eastern Europe.

CHAPTER TEN

Leisure Time
in Delaware

Delaware's location is great for business, and it's great for leisure time activities too. No Delawarean need travel far to enjoy the best in the arts and sport. Some of the best is found right at home.

The Penmen

The most significant writer in Delaware history was John Dickinson, who is known as the Penman of the Revolution. In the 1760s when England was passing many laws to try to bring the colonies more firmly under its control, he wrote essays that appeared in many newspapers and helped turn the public against England. Later he helped write the Articles of Confederation and the U.S. Constitution.

Pulitzer Prize-winner John P. Marquand was a native of Wilmington.

Writer Robert Montgomery Bird was born in New Castle in 1806. A physician, he wrote plays, such as *The Gladiator*, that were popular in both the United States and England. He later turned to novels, such as *Hawks of Hawk Hollow,* about America's early years in the frontier locales he explored. His novels, too, were popular at home and overseas.

Twentieth-century novelist John P. Marquand was a native of Wilmington, born in 1893. He wrote about life among the upper class, especially in New England, where he went to live as a young man. Several of his novels were made into movies. The most

Opposite: Building a sandcastle at Bethany Beach

Music in Wilmington

Wilmington's Grand Opera House (above) on the Market Street Mall began life in 1871 as a theater and masonic hall. It was brought into existence with the encouragement of some of the city's industrialists. The building, which has an ornate cast-iron facade, is home to the Delaware Centre for the Performing Arts, Opera-Delaware, and the Delaware Symphony. ∎

famous is *Point of No Return. The Late George Apley* won a Pulitzer Prize in 1938. He also invented the popular Japanese spy Mr. Moto.

Henry Seidel Canby, born in Wilmington in 1878, was the founder of the *Saturday Review of Literature*. For many decades, he and his staff decreed, by their reviews and comments, what the American public should read and the plays it should see.

The Illustrators

Dover's Samuel C. Biggs Musem of American Art has a fine collection of paintings by American artists. One room celebrates to the work of Frank Schoonover, one of the Brandywine illustrators.

The Brandywine School is the name given to a group of artists who worked in Delaware and nearby Pennsylvania. They were primarily illustrators, doing paintings intended to be used for book illustrations, but today their work is regarded as fine art.

The founder of the Brandywine School was artist Howard Pyle, born in Wilmington in 1853. He wrote and illustrated many children's books, including the still-popular *The Merrie Adventures of Robin Hood* and *Otto of the Silver Hand*. He ran a school for illustrators in his Wilmington studio.

Probably his greatest student was N. C. (Newell Convers) Wyeth, a Massachusetts-born artist who joined Pyle when he was twenty and remained with him for many years. Wyeth created many magazine covers, as well as perhaps 3,000 illustrations for books, including many children's classics such as *Treasure Island*, *Kidnapped*, and *Last of the Mohicans*. He, in turn, taught what he had learned from Pyle to his son, Andrew, who is today known as perhaps America's greatest twentieth-century painter. Many of Andrew Wyeth paintings hang in the Hotel du Pont in Wilmington. N. C.'s grandson, Jamie, has done many fine paintings, particularly of the Brandywine area.

Howard Pyle was influential in the Brandywine School.

Jamie Wyeth, part of a famous family of artists, is a renowned painter.

Racing to Glory

Delaware Park, a thoroughbred horse racetrack, opened at Stanton near Wilmington in 1937. In the spring, the grounds of Winterthur are used for steeplechase races, which involve jumps rather than speed. During fall

A dawn workout at Delaware Park

and winter, a track at Dover Downs is used for harness racing. In this form of racing, horses pull lightweight two-wheeled carts called sulkies.

Dover Downs International Speedway, which is within an easy drive of several major cities, is more often used for car racing. Racing fans head there to watch the NASCAR events being driven on the Monster Mile. The big 200-mile and 400-mile events are sponsored by MBNA, the banking firm headquartered in Wilmington. Indy car racing in the form of the Delaware 500 is also held on the Monster Mile.

A totally different kind of racing has been the Tour du Pont, held on several different occasions in the 1990s. This is a twelve-day, 1,600-km professional cycling race. In 1996, the winner was Lance Armstrong, the cyclist who three years later overcame cancer to win the 1999 Tour de France in Europe.

The name du Pont is also important in golf. The Du Pont Country Club in Delaware is the site of one of the courses used by the Ladies' Professional Golf Association championship tour.

At the Beaches

One popular outdoor activity in Delaware is fishing. While most places aren't really good for night fishing, there's a pier in Cape

A Different Kind of Contest

Every farmer who grows pumpkins has a lot left over—there's a limit to how many jack-o'-lanterns can be made. In 1985, two youths in Lewes, Trey Melson and Bill Thompson, challenged a friend to a pumpkin-throwing contest. The three teams who took part were allowed to use anything they could find to toss the pumpkins—machines built from pulleys and garage door springs were popular. That year, the winning distance for the *Punkin' Chuck* championship was 128 feet, 2 inches (39 m). In 1998, the event had grown to twenty-seven competing teams, watched by more than 25,000 spectators in a two-day event. The winning distance in 1998 was 3,718 feet (1,134 m). ■

Henlopen State Park that stretches far out into the bay. Fishing enthusiasts go there day or night.

Many beaches on the east coast are as popular for fishing as for swimming and sand-castle building. The enthusiasts stand on the beach and cast out into the surf, hoping to hook some of the many

Boating and fishing are popular pastimes in Delaware.

fish that linger just out of sight, feeding on the many small critters that gather near the shore. Broadkill Beach between Lewes and Milford has a special attraction. Huge numbers of fish gather there to feed in a peculiar dip in the shallow water during spring when the water is warming up.

At some Delaware state parks, people have to climb sand dunes to get to the beach.

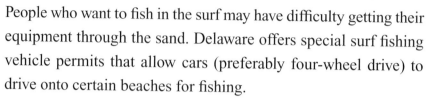

A Record Fish

The international records for most ocean fish were won in warm waters far from the East Coast, but the biggest fish—the black drum—was caught at Lewes in 1975. That fish weighed in at 113 pounds 1 ounce (51 kg). The black drum, which is actually grayish red, is related to the whiting, bluefish, and weakfish. ■

People who want to fish in the surf may have difficulty getting their equipment through the sand. Delaware offers special surf fishing vehicle permits that allow cars (preferably four-wheel drive) to drive onto certain beaches for fishing.

Lewes is the setting-off point for many people's adventures in deep-sea fishing. They catch marlin and tuna in the Atlantic Ocean.

Delaware health authorities monitor the pollution levels at the state's beaches and warn swimmers when the water might not be safe. Also, when red flags are out, authorities warn that the surf is dangerous and swimming is not permitted.

Sailing and speedboating are ever-popular sports in the bay and in the Atlantic. Recently, kayaking in the bays along Delaware's beaches has gained favor as a water sport.

Baseball Comes Home

Wilmington saw its first professional baseball in 1883, though the popular Diamond State team had been playing for twenty years. Over the following years, several pro teams played, but they never quite made it into the major leagues. That didn't bother Delawareans, though, where the fans remained faithful to the on-again, off-again schedule of the minor-league teams.

The Fightin' Blue Hens

The University of Delaware's sports teams are called the Fightin' Blue Hens. In football, Delaware belongs to the Atlantic 10 Conference. In basketball, University of Delaware was the America East Conference champ in 1997–98. At football and basketball games, the cheering spectators are urged on by a giant chicken (left)—blue, of course—that is said to wear a size 28FF shoe. ■

Landfall Park, the new home of the Blue Rocks

The most successful twentieth-century team was the Blue Rocks, formed in 1939 as the farm team of the Philadelphia Athletics and then the Phillies. But television killed the minor leagues in the early 1950s, and the Blue Rocks disappeared, until 1993, when a new ballpark in south Wilmington opened with the new Blue Rocks as the home team.

Timeline

United States History

The first permanent English settlement is established in North America at Jamestown. **1607**

Pilgrims found Plymouth Colony, the second permanent English settlement. **1620**

America declares its independence from Britain. **1776**

The Treaty of Paris officially ends the Revolutionary War in America. **1783**

The U.S. Constitution is written. **1787**

The Louisiana Purchase almost doubles the size of the United States. **1803**

The United States and Britain **1812–15** fight the War of 1812.

Delaware State History

1609 Henry Hudson discovers what is now called Delaware Bay.

1610 Sameul Argall gives the name "Cape De La Warr" to what is now Cape Henlopen.

1631 Dutch settlers establish a colony call Zwaanendael.

1638 Swedish settlers found the colony o New Sweden.

1655 Peter Stuyvesant seizes New Swede for the Dutch West India Company.

1664 The English capture all the Dutch settlements in Delaware.

1682 William Penn takes over Delaware counties.

1704 Delaware's first independent legislature convenes.

1776 Delegates from the three Delaware counties organize a state governmen

1787 Delaware becomes the first state of t Union on December 7.

1802 A gunpowder mill is established nea Wilmington by Eleuthère-Irénée du Pont de Nemours.

United States History

The North and South fight **1861–65**
th other in the American Civil War.

The United States is **1917–18**
involved in World War I.

The stock market crashes, **1929**
plunging the United States into
the Great Depression.

The United States **1941–45**
fights in World War II.
The United States becomes a **1945**
charter member of the U.N.

The United States **1951–53**
fights in the Korean War.

e U.S. Congress enacts a series of **1964**
groundbreaking civil rights laws.

The United States **1964–73**
engages in the Vietnam War.

The United States and other **1991**
nations fight the brief
Persian Gulf War against Iraq.

Delaware State History

1829 The Chesapeake and Delaware Canal
opens between Chesapeake and
Delaware Bays.

1897 Delaware ratifies its current
constitution.

1924 The DuPont Parkway is opened and
given to the state.

1951 The Delaware Memorial Bridge
connects New Jersey and Delaware.

1971 The Coastal Zone Act prohibits future
industrial construction along the coast.

1987 Delaware celebrates the bicentennial
of its statehood.

1999 The Delaware Commerative quarter
is issued.

Fast Facts

Legislative Hall

Statehood date	December 7, 1787; the 1st state
Origin of state name	Named for Lord De La Warr, early governor of Delaware. Originally the name was applied to the river, then to the Indian tribe (Lenape) and the state.
State capital	Dover
State nickname	Diamond State, First State, Blue Hen State
State motto	Liberty and Independence
State bird	Blue hen chicken
State flower	Peach blossom
State insect	Ladybug
State fish	Weakfish
State mineral	Sillimanite
State song	"Our Delaware"
State tree	American holly

Blue hen chicken

State beverage	Milk
State colors	Colonial blue and buff
State fair	Harrington (end of July)
Total area; rank	2,397 sq. mi. (6,208 sq km); 49th
Land; rank	1,955 sq. mi. (5,063 sq km); 49th
Water; rank	442 sq. mi. (1,145 sq km); 41st
Inland water; **rank**	71 sq. mi. (184 sq km); 49th
Coastal water; **rank**	371 sq. mi. (960 sq km); 15th
Geographic center	Kent, 11 miles (18 km) south of Dover
Latitude and longitude	Delaware is located approximately between 38° 27' and 45° 05' N and 75° 03' and 75° 47' W
Highest point	Ebright Road in New Castle County, 442 feet (135 m)
Lowest point	Sea level at the coast
Largest city	Wilmington
Number of counties	3
Population; rank	668,696 (1990 census); 46th
Density	330 persons per sq. mi. (127 per sq km)
Population distribution	73% urban, 27% rural

Wilmington

Ethnic distribution (does not equal 100%)	
White	80.32%
African-American	16.88%
Hispanic	2.37%
Asian and Pacific Islanders	1.36%
Native American	0.30%
Other	1.13%

Record high temperature	110°F (43°C) at Millsboro on July 21, 1930
Record low temperature	−17°F (−27°C) at Millsboro on January 17, 1893
Average July temperature	76°F (24°C)
Average January temperature	35°F (2°C)
Average annual precipitation	45 inches (114 cm)

Cape Henlopen State Park

Natural Areas and Historic Sites

State Parks

Delaware has thirteen state parks.

Sports Teams

NCAA Teams (Division 1)

Delaware State University Hornets

University of Delaware Fightin' Blue Hens

Cultural Institutions

Libraries

The *University of Delaware Library* (Newark) has a highly regarded collection on Delaware's history as well as a 2,000-volume collection of books on the public and private life of Abraham Lincoln.

Delaware State Archives (Dover) and the *Delaware State Historical Society* (Wilmington) both have fine collections on Delaware history.

The *Eleutherian Mills-Hagley Foundation* (Greenville) has a noted collection on American economic history.

Delaware Art Museum

Museums

The *Henry Francis du Pont Winterthur Museum* (Wilmington) has an excellent collection of American decorative arts.

The *Hagley Museum and Eleutherian Mills* (Wilmington) offers exhibits featuring industrial life in the 1800s.

The *Delaware State Museum* (Dover) fills three buildings and features exhibits on the state's culture and history.

Performing Arts

Delaware has one major opera company and one major orchestra.

Universities and Colleges

In the late 1990s, Delaware had five public and four private institutions of higher learning.

Annual Events

January–March

Delaware Kite Festival at Cape Henlopen State Park in Lewes (Good Friday)

Boardwalk Fashion Promenade at Rehoboth Beach (Easter Sunday)

April–June

Irish Festival at Hagley Museum near Wilmington (last Saturday in April)

Great Delaware Kite Festival at Cape Henlopen (late April)

Old Dover Days (first Saturday in May)

Wilmington Garden Day in Wilmington (first Saturday in May)

Winterthur Point to Point Horse Race (first Sunday in May)

Tour du Pont bicycle race (early May)

A Day in Old New Castle (May)

McDonald's LPGA Golf Championship in Wilmington (Spring)

Miller 500 stock car race in Dover (June)

At the Delmar Dragway

Delaware state fair

July–September

Rockwood's Victorian Ice Cream Festival, Wilmington (July)

Delaware State Fair in Harrington (July)

Bethany Beach Boardwalk Arts Festival (August)

Nanticoke Indian Pow Wow near Oak Orchard (second week in September)

Brandywine Arts Festival in Wilmington (second Saturday in September)

MBNA 400 stock car race in Dover (September)

October–December

Delaware Decoy Festival and Carving Championship in Odessa (October)

Fall Harvest Festival at the Delaware Agricultural Museum in Dover (late October)

Candlelight tours of historic homes in Newcastle (December)

Christmas and Candlelight tours at nine museums in the Brandywine Valley (December)

Famous People

James Asheton Bayard (1767–1815)	Diplomat and statesman
James Asheton Bayard (1799–1880)	Lawyer and U.S. senator
Emily Bissell (1861–1948)	introduced Christmas seals
Henry Seidel Canby (1878–1961)	Author and publisher
Annie Jump Cannon (1863–1941)	Astronomer
John Middleton Clayton (1796–1856)	U.S. senator and U.S. secretary of state

Alfred I. du Pont

Alfred Irénée du Pont (1864–1935)	Industrialist and philanthropist
Henry du Pont (1812–1889)	Industrialist
Henry Algernon du Pont (1838–1926)	Politician and industrialist
Pierre Samuel du Pont (1870–1954)	Industrialist and philanthropist
T. Coleman du Pont (1863–1930)	Industrialist; builder of Route 13/DuPont Highway
Thomas Garrett (1789–1871)	Abolitionist and Underground Railroad conductor
Jacob Jones (1768–1850)	Naval officer
Thomas Macdonough (1783–1825)	Naval officer
John Phillips Marquand (1893–1960)	Author
Howard Pyle (1853–1911)	Author and artist
Caesar Rodney (1728–1784)	Patriot and statesman

Howard Pyle

To Find Out More

History

- Brown, Dottie. *Delaware*. Minneapolis: Lerner, 1994.

- Fradin, Dennis Brindell. *Delaware*. Chicago: Childrens Press, 1995.

- Fradin, Dennis Brindell. *The Delaware Colony*. Chicago: Childrens Press, 1992.

- Thompson, Kathleen. *Delaware*. Austin, Tex.: Raintree/Steck Vaughn, 1996.

- Wilker, Josh. *The Lenape Indians*. Broomall, Penn.: Chelsea House, 1994.

Biographies

- Lutz, Norma Jean. *William Penn*. Broomall, Penn.: Chelsea House, 1999.

- Rangel, Fernando. *Beyond the Sea of Ice: Voyages of Henry Hudson*. Toronto: Firefly Books, 1999.

- Schlesinger, Arthur M., Jr. *Peter Stuyvesant: Dutch Military Leader*. Broomall, Penn.: Chelsea House, 1999.

Fiction

- Keehn, Sally M. *The Moon of Two Dark Horses*. New York: Philomel Books, 1995.

- Laird, Marnie. *Water Rat*. Oxfordshire, U.K.: Winslow Press, 1998.

Website

- **State of Delaware**

  http://www.state.de.us/

  The official website for the state of Delaware

Addresses

- **Delaware Tourism Office**

  99 Kings Highway

  P.O. Box 1401

  Dover, DE 19903

  For information about Delaware's tourism, economy, government, and history

- **Delaware State Parks**

  89 Kings Highway

  P.O. Box 1401

  Dover, DE 19903

  For information about Delaware state parks

Index

Page numbers in *italics* indicate illustrations.

Meet the Author

Jean Blashfield lived in northern Virginia for several years while working in Washington, D.C., and became fascinated by the ever-present history of the original thirteen colonies on the East Coast. She made many trips throughout the region.

During many years in publishing, Blashfield developed several encyclopedias, including *Young People's Science Encyclopedia* for Children's Press. While living in Arlington, Virginia, she opened offices for Funk & Wagnalls to create a general encyclopedia for young students.

In addition to living in Virginia, she has lived and worked in Chicago; London, England; and Washington, D.C. But when she married Wallace Black (a Chicago publisher, writer, and pilot), they moved to Wisconsin. Today, she has two college-age children and lives in Delavan, Wisconsin.

Jean Blashfield has written about ninety books, most of them for young people. She likes best to write about interesting places, but she loves history and science, too. She becomes fascinated by just about every subject she investigates. She has created an encyclopedia of aviation and space, written popular books on murderers and house plants, and had a lot of fun creating an early book on the things women have done called *Hellraisers, Heroines, and Holy Women.*

In Wisconsin, she delighted in finding TSR, Inc., the publishers of the *Dungeons & Dragons* games. At that company, she founded a new department to publish fantasy books and helped the company expand into a worldwide enterprise.

Photo Credits